Resolving Yesterday - First Aid for Stress and Trauma with TTT

Resolving Yesterday

First Aid for Stress and Trauma with TTT

Gunilla Hamne & Ulf Sandström

Publishing Statement
This book is also available on our website in a simplified electronic version.
Proceeds from book sales are used to fund books for somebody who cannot afford it but needs it.

Resolving Yesterday
First Aid for Stress and Trauma with TTT
Gunilla Hamne & Ulf Sandström

ISBN-13: 978-1505832990

Photos: Photos: Gunilla Hamne & Ulf Sandström, except page 64 Diane Cowel
Illustrations: Mats Ottosson, Kalle Johansson (page 193) and Benard Githogori (page 192)
Graphic Design cover: Per Thorsell, Vitt Grafiska AB
Graphic Design inlay: Marina Wiking, www.marinawiking.se
Print: Amazon

Resolving Yesterday - First Aid for Stress and Trauma with TTT

About this book

"It's no secret that we live in a stress-filled world. In fact, stress is such a common theme of conversation that most people act as if it is just part of life and that nothing can, or even should be done about it. Even then, there is an almost universal pessimism about the possibility of overcoming the devastating consequences of stress caused by severe conditions such as armed conflict, mass murders including genocide, or catastrophic natural disasters such as hurricane, tornado, earthquake, tsunami, flash flooding or forest fire".

Bert Fellows, PhD, MA

This book explains some of the causes of emotional and post-traumatic stress, and the physical and psychological symptoms it can lead to. It provides a First Aid technique to heal the symptoms that is called the Trauma Tapping Technique, TTT. TTT is easy enough to be learned by children, yet powerful enough to astound psychologists, psychiatrists and counselors as well as long time sufferers of trauma.

In this book we will tell how you can use TTT to
- Treat yourself
- Treat others
- Teach and treat large groups of people that can spread it even further

There are three different ways of presenting TTT
- As a relaxation method in school or health care. Before a game of chess or a public presentation.
- As an add-on to therapy, coaching, counselling you are already doing.
- As an intervention at workplaces, groups and organizations.

Allow it to spread through ripples of healing. Pass it on. Pay it forward. This book is our contribution to peace, since we believe that peace starts in each and every one of us.

Gunilla Hamne on the way to a TTT workshop in Rwanda.

About Us

Gunilla Hamne:
At one point in life, I was working internationally as a journalist and filmmaker with focus on environmental issues and human rights. I came to visit many places and interviewed people who had been traumatized by war, genocide and natural disasters.

I did not feel comfortable. Something was missing, but I didn't know what. My turning point was in the shade under a mango tree with Ahok, a 12 year old Dinka girl in Marial Bai, a village-like town in what is now South Sudan. It was in 2003 and the liberation war with the north part of Sudan was still going on.

Ahok was telling me how she was abducted when she was eight years old and the village was attacked by the militia from the north of the country. They came on horses, burned, looted, killed and forced her and other children and women to go with them to be used as slaves. She was a slave for three years until she was finally rescued.

I asked her for the details I needed to compose a vivid story: "How were the militia men dressed? What time of the day was it? How did it smell at the market where they sold you? What did they say to you? What happened to your parents? Did you see them being killed? What did it look like along the road?"

Ahok told me everything that I wanted to know. While talking she looked down on the ground, drawing lines in the sand with a stick.

In that moment an uncomfortable feeling lingered in my body. I would get my story. But something else worried me: What would happen to Ahok when I leave her with the memories that I have made vivid again, reminding her of her trauma with all my questions?

A thought came to my mind: "I don't want to take another story from people who suffer and leave them with the pain."

I knew it is important to write about atrocities and people's sufferings to be able to raise awareness about different issues as in this case of child slavery. This was not the problem. But to get the stories I had to ask re-traumatizing questions without having anything to offer to ease the pain I caused.

When I went back to South Sudan ten years later, in 2013, it was an independent nation, I was able to teach people how to deal with their traumas of war and slavery.

The tool for my own personal change and what made all our work today possible was a training in TFT, Thought Field Therapy. TFT is the original tapping technique invented by Dr. Roger Callahan. In the handouts there was one article that caught my interest more than anything else. It was an article about five psychologists who had been using tapping in Kosovo to assist people who had been traumatized during the Balkan wars in the late 1990's. I thought to myself: "This is what I have to do. I will go to places where the need for trauma relief is great but recourses are small or none existent, and teach tapping."

Because, if that technique was as good as it was portrayed to be, it had to be spread.

A bold email makes a big difference

Gunilla continues:

I could not do it alone. I needed somebody who could teach me how to work with severe traumas. A mentor. I got the names of the authors of the article about Kosovo and started searching for them on the internet. After some time I managed to get the email address for the main author of the article: Professor of psychology and trauma expert for 25 years, Dr. Carl Johnson from Virginia in the US. I wrote what became the email that changed my life; a naïve and kind of funny email. It went like this:

"Dear Carl,
I am writing to you since I have read about the fantastic work you have been doing with TFT in Kosovo. I have myself quite recently finished the TFT training here in Sweden. I am now practicing as much as I can.
Through my other work (I am also a journalist) I have been in contact with many organizations, especially in the South working with children's rights and victims of war. So, since I finished this TFT education I have had the goal to use this relieving tool of tapping in those places where I have been as a journalist. I

would like to give some peace of mind to the children who have suffered. And give the TFT tool to community leaders for it to expand. That would be a further step from just writing about people's difficulties. I now wonder if you have any new missions planned and if it would be possible for me to participate? Or if not, do you have any good advices, how I can go further? I am very used to traveling and living under simple conditions. I have a deep and good feeling for people. Thank you so much for your help. Hope to hear from you.

Gunilla Hamne, Stockholm, Sweden"

To my big surprise Dr. Johnson replied within some days. He wrote:

"Dear Gunilla

How pleasant it is to receive your letter. I am very open to suggestions and to your thoughts about places in need. I am most open to being pushed toward somewhere that suffers desperately. I have no missions planned, but if you have some suggestions I am willing to go. Just give me some six months to earn for the ticket and prepare myself.

So much can be done to comfort agony. I have worked with terrorists and seen their hate replaced by love. It is possible to enhance self-esteem in people who think they have nothing, and it is possible to bring peace to places that have never experienced it, in any place.

But it is essential to be humble and to recognize the healing powers within each person... and assign all credit for the healing to the patient therefore.

I am sure we should go to the most hopeless places, do the seemingly impossible projects... for nothing will prove impossible at all if God is with us...and he always is."

Six months later, Dr. Johnson and I went to Rwanda. In Rwanda I contacted AOCM – an organization of child headed households: in effect, orphans of the genocide living together forming new families since their parents all had been killed. I came to know their chairman and founder Naphtal Ahishakiye when he received the World's Children's Prize in Sweden in 2006. They were happy to get training for their members in trauma treatment. Dr. Carl Johnson had been to Rwanda before and felt comfortable going there again.

We started out working with a group of 15 young orphans, most of them in their 20's. We had the trainings in the house of one of the orphan families in the housing project of Kiyninya, just outside Kigali. Kiyninya is like a suburban village on a hillside with around 200 identical houses built for widows and orphans. If you come there it probably looks idyllic, green and calm. Pine trees, banana plants and maize. You might look over to the next green hill and the valley down below. At that time, during the nights, many of the houses were filled with nightmares of fearful memories.

When the participants of the trainings had been treated and had learned the tapping technique they went to ask if any of the neighbors wanted to try. Many volunteered. Off we went the whole group, walking to the clients' houses to practice the treatment with them.

From this first group of trainees deep relations came to grow with some of the participants who later became our guides in to the Rwandese language, culture and society. Without them we would never have reached so far and understood as much as we have been able to. This goes specifically for Robert Ntabwoba, Jacques Sezikeye and Murigo Veneranda (you will meet them in the book). They are today part of the network of Trauma Tappers that we call Peaceful Heart Network.

When Dr Johnson and I met Robert Ntabwoba the first time, he was very sceptic. *"I though it looked stupid this tapping thing, stupid and ridiculous. But I though by the end of the day we would get paid for being in the training"*, he thought. After being treated and waking up the next day he realized that his nightmares were gone. There had been no killers in his room that night. When he came back to the training the day after, he said:

"I didn´t know I was traumatized, but it seems this tapping has cured me from those uncomfortable feelings I thought was part of me. I will be here when you come next time. I want to help you to spread this method." And so he did.

We worked extensively together in Rwanda. Later we got invited to other countries in African as well as Europe and Canada. Bringing our different life experiences and backgrounds into the trainings was a big advantage for acceptance and understanding of the method.

Many have joined our cause along the way, making Peaceful Heart Network grow through these personal experiences of healing.

Ulf Sandström:
I found TTT because I ran into a language barrier working as a hypnotherapist and a coach.

At the time I was helping clients resolve all kinds of emotional imbalances, many of them due to traumas in childhood that were retriggered at a later point in life. I met a lot of people who wanted to resolve emotional reactions to memories of sexual abuse, intimidation and acts of violence that had happened over 10-40 years earlier – and still affected them negatively.

With the tools of hypnotherapy and Neuro Linguistic Programming (NLP) there are wonderful ways of resolving theses symptoms. However, these methods are completely language dependent and some of my clients spoke very limited Swedish and English. I started wondering if there might be a different way to calm the fight-or-flight center of the brain without talking?

I started looking into every way of resolving conditioned stress responses I could find. My research led me to the blog of Gunilla Hamne who was traveling around in Africa, helping people with emotional and traumatic stress without the need for language dependent interventions. It said she was teaching those who were treated to treat others, passing it on. I had found the Peaceful Heart Network and Trauma Tapping. Could this be true? Why hadn't I heard of it earlier?

Another email makes a big difference
"Hi Gunilla
I read you fantastic blog and I want to learn this to teach others. I have travelled extensively in many parts of the world and I am a certified hypnotherapist and able to treat, for example phobias and anxiety, but it doesn't work over language barriers, what you are doing seems to work for trauma and phobias regardless of language?

Can we find a way for me to learn from you?
Ulf Sandström, Stockholm, Sweden"

A couple of months later Gunilla and her colleague Robert Ntabwoba arrived in Stockholm and we decided to meet up so they could train me, and my wife, Melodie.

The first thing I noticed when Robert was tapping my wife was that the technique was simple, elegant and efficient – beyond my expectations. No suffering, no delving into details, lots of integrity and calm: just the touch of fingertips tapping on specific points. My wife´s father had just passed away in cancer, and the session released a lot of the tensions in a smooth way. Was this the tool for resolving emotional and post-traumatic stress without spoken interventions that I had been looking for?

My analytical and skeptical mind was creating a list of questions:
- So, how does it work, exactly?
- How do you know the results are permanent?
- What is the science behind it?
- Are there any clinical studies?
- How do we know it isn't a placebo effect?
- How do we present this to those who need it?
- Why is it not a standard First Aid intervention?

I have put Trauma Tapping to every test I could think of. I have integrated it with hypnotherapy in many different ways, and I used it as an intervention of its own. I have tried it on people with open minds to alternative medicine and also with those who laughed at it and thought it looked silly. The results were persistently positive within reason, and beyond expectations.

When Gunilla and Robert went back to Rwanda two months later they asked if I wanted to join them on location, which I did gladly. In Rwanda I experienced that healing really is possible, teaching TTT to groups of survivors of the genocide. I also noticed that treating and teaching TTT in combination with musical interaction as it is done, was a method in itself – then I knew this was the right thing for me to be doing, having been a professional musician since I was fifteen. I joined the Peaceful Heart Network as a co-founder the same year, to bring this tool to those who need it most.

If you are already involved in therapy of some sort and looking for a very useful addition, or if you would like just one single tool that can make a difference for any person experiencing emotional or post-traumatic stress, this is a great one: TTT!

Ulf Sandström after a workshop at Cuyve on the border between Rwanda and Congo.

Eugénie Mukamazimpaka in Kiziguro, Rwanda, a women's group organizer.

Acknowledgements

This book is dedicated to the survivors of unimaginable acts of war, genocide, and emotional distress of all kinds that we have met in Chad, Rwanda, Afghanistan, Uganda, Sierra Leone, Congo, Canada, Finland, South Sudan, Sweden and many other countries, thank you for your trust in allowing us to teach you how to treat yourselves and your community, thank you for proving to us that Trauma Tapping Technique (TTT) is one of the most useful tools around today for shutting down traumatic stress responses. You have shown us that healing is possible.

A special thanks to Dr. Carl Johnson without whom the development of TTT would never had happened, and our brothers and sisters in Rwanda; Robert Ntabwoba, Murigo Veneranda, Jacques Sezikeye, Godelieve Mukasarasi and Didacienne Mukahabeshimana, for your incredible efforts and inspiration. Unlimited thanks to our colleagues in Congo Germando Barathi and Amani Matabaro, the young women, Christine Shuler Deschryver and the rest of the staff at City of Joy, the artistic children at ASO, the former child soldiers, staff and Murhabazi Namegabe at BVES. And all our trauma tappers: Salim Rajani in Afghanistan, Cherif Choukou and Clément Abaifouta in Chad, John Njoroge and Emmily Korir in Kenya, Ajing Chol Giir and Maketh Kuot Deng in South Sudan, Masu Sesay and Lilian Morsay in Sierra Leone, and everybody else we have met and shared the TTT with. Thanks also to Alan Channer, Dr. Pastor James Wuye, Dr. Imam Muhammad Ashafa, Florrie Widén, Göran Gunér, Mia Hallberg, Maj Stoddard, Gerard Osenele Ukpan, Åsa Ottosson, Mats Ottoson, Martina Lindroos, Fredrik Praesto, Nils Ola Nilsson, Benoit Charlebois, Rob Nelson, our fantastic layout artist Marina Wiking, warm thanks for efforts to Tom Oberbichler, Chris Pape, Michelle Campbell-Scott, Bert Fellows, John Grinder, Ronald Ruden, Melodie Sandström, Annika McKillen, Agneta Sandström, Moa Hamne, Anders Sandström and the rest of our friends and families, and our wonderfully persistent proofreader Anna G. Hildenbrand Wachtmeister. If you are not mentioned in print you are most probably mentioned on our website, and definitely imprinted in our hearts.

With love,
Gunilla Hamne and *Ulf Sandström*

Table of Contents

About this book	5
About Us	7
Acknowledgements	15
Forewords	19
The Structure of This Book	27

WHAT IS TTT?	**29**
First Aid for Emotional and Traumatic Stress	31
The Evolution of TTT	35
Presenting Trauma Tapping	39
A Little Bird	40

SELF HELP WITH TTT	**43**
The Trauma Tapping Technique (TTT)	45
Self Tapping Step by Step	46

OFFERING A TTT SESSION	**49**
Who Can Be Treated?	51
Before a Session	52
During A Session	58
After A Session	60
Now Try!	65
Tapping Somebody Step by Step	66
Helping Children	69
Marie – A Session in Rwanda	72
TTT over Skype	74
Teaching TTT on the Fly	77
Using TTT with Hypnotherapy	82
Metaphors of Healing	84
The Dizziness Disappeared	87

TTT WITH GROUPS	**89**
The Starfish Thrower	90
Teaching and Treating in Groups	93
The Somatic Poem	97
Trauma Tapping in Song and Dance	99
Fatumeh, a Survivor of Sexual Violence	106
The Invisible Beauty of TTT	109
"Nobody Offered Us Healing"	114

UNDERSTANDING STRESS	**117**
Mechanics of Stress and Trauma	119
The Encoding and Decoding of Trauma	123
Emotions, Thoughts and Behaviors	127
Signs of Emotional and Traumatic Stress	131
Surviving Sexual Abuse	134
Children as Weapons of War	137
Possession by Demons	142
First Time in 34 Years	143
A Mindset for Survival	145
Caring in a Good Way	149
Picking up Emotions	151
Resilience to Trauma	152
An Overview of PTSD Treatments	155
ADDITIONAL TECHNIQUES	**159**
Emotional Body-Techniques	160
Crown Pull	161
Gorilla Tapping Relief	162
Soothing Head Holding	163
Alpha-Theta Breathing	164
Balancing the Brain	165
Do-in Self Massage	166
Aggression Blow-Out	168
Energizing Power Posing	169
The Pathfinder Cards	170
PEACEFUL HEART NETWORK	**173**
Our Vision	175
Building Peace	176
To Ease Suffering and Prevent Violence	179
What We do and Why	181
Trauma Tapping Centers	183
Certified Trauma Tapper	187
Spreading the News	191
The Multiplying Effect	194
Healing, and then what?	198
A WIDER PERSPECTIVE	**201**
A Wider Perspective	203
Disclaimer	207
Glossary	208
Index	224
Books for references and inspiration	226

Resolving Yesterday - First Aid for Stress and Trauma with TTT

Road view between workshops in Kerala, India.

Forewords

Bert Fellows, MA
Director Emeritus, Psychological Services
Pain Management Center of Paducah, USA

What Gunilla and Ulf have masterfully done through their years of hands-on experience with the most complex of Post Traumatic Stress cases is to refine various tapping techniques into a revolutionary interventional first-aid technique that brings hope to the hopeless and self-empowerment to the powerless. They have named it the Trauma Tapping Technique (TTT), an emotional first-aid technique that is, on the one hand, so amazingly simple, straightforward and versatile, while on the other hand, so powerful and effective as to free even the most traumatized individual from their suffering and despair, sometimes within a single 15–25 minute session, sometimes, miraculously, in even fewer minutes.

These spectacularly consistent results defy all expectations of the rational, logical, traditional mind-set which cries out, "impossible"! But Ulf and Gunilla's results speak otherwise and affirm that these results are not only possible but probable. It reminds one of how it was once believed that to run the mile in under 4 minutes was deemed impossible until Roger Bannister came along in 1954 and for the first time ran a mile in under 4 minutes. Since that barrier was broken, it has become commonplace to run the mile in under 4 minutes. Likewise, rapid remediation of severe trauma will become commonplace as the world becomes aware that the barrier of impossibility to speedy and permanent trauma relief has been torn down and TTT has been at the forefront of this evolution.

What is more, they have emphasized and demonstrated the teachability of TTT through group interventions in such a way as to bypass cultural and language barriers and to repeatedly communicate to their audiences that they are teaching them to help themselves, that once taught they no longer need the teachers. Their language is always about self-empowerment, self sufficiency and self-efficacy, and always delivered with wit and good humor even in the most serious situations.

TTT is a beautiful technique that is firmly and simply structured but not bound by any rigid, dogmatic procedural rules. Rather, it goes with the flow of circumstances in the service of being compassionately present and more concerned about honoring the individual rather than any strict treatment objective. It is a wonderful example of being adaptively, creatively flexible. The outcome is self-empowerment of the highest order as evidenced by the many poignant stories of triumph over trauma.

In this highly complicated and stressed-out world, we are in great need of simple self-management tools which offer solutions. The vast majority of us are always looking for such tools to improve our lives, but we are so busy we want only those that are the most cutting-edge, effective, tested, proven, easy to learn, rapid, portable and affordable. Because it is the Information Age that we live in, we are flooded by offers of such tools advertised to us incessantly from every side and the challenge becomes one of sifting through the sand for the nuggets of Gold. TTT is one such nugget.

Whether you are a social worker, psychologist, psychiatrist, mental health counselor or other health and human services provider working for a governmental organization or privately, or you want to use this technique as a volunteer to help any needy and willing person, you will find TTT to be a useful, effective and easy to learn, practical tool. You can even use it on yourself and that is probably the most important place to start so that you will know from your own experience how magical it can be. If you need a bit more than the book itself contains, don't worry, as *The Peaceful Heart Network* website has plenty of additional information including links to YouTube demonstrations and other resources.

If you are looking for a life changing tool that is simple, has minimal requirements, is easily transferable with minimal to no language/cultural barrier, easily multiplied through group treatments and trainings, that emphasizes self-empowerment, then the Trauma Tapping Technique is for you and this book is your access to it.

Get your start here and begin the journey. You won't be sorry you did.

John Grinder
Co-creator of Neuro-Linguistic Programming

It is horrifying to experience the violence of war. And as many people can attest, these experiences often persist, dragging the survivor out of their present and back into the reliving of what they survived. Such living in the past, such powerful regressions into re-experiencing what they suffered, means that their present experience is filtered through the unconscious re-activation of their past defeats. They must make a huge effort to put that past behind them and move with grace and strength into a future of their own choosing and design.

They are trapped in the cage of their own personal history – their daily experience distorted through the prism of their past, corrupted by things that they did not choose. They survived the horrors of war only to find themselves imprisoned in the memories of what they managed to live through.

The question is how to help such people to liberate themselves from these re-occurring experiences that dominate their post trauma experiences. Fortunately, there are many choices about how to do this – many patterns of intervention that have done well can offer the assistance that these people seek. Unfortunately, people well-trained in the application of these intervention patterns are most typically not available to precisely the people who most need them.

I have witnessed the work of Gunilla Hamne and her colleague Ulf Sandström in demonstrations of their tapping protocols, one of the many intervention patterns on offer for accomplishing such work I have received from them and others most positive reports of their work in different parts of the world, and especially in parts of Africa, parts that have suffered genocidal wars.

These reports lead me to endorse the work that they and their colleagues are doing. Their work has touched the lives of many people in a most positive way. And sensitive to the cultural differences between their home culture (Scandinavian) and the diverse cultures of the different parts of Africa, they have in conjunction with their African colleagues developed some intervention forms (rhythm, movement and song) that support and intensify their tapping methodology that they apply. I deeply respect their commitment and most positive intentions in bringing relief to the people of Africa from the ravages of recent wars and traumas.

***

Carl Johnson, PhD

Horrifying events happen every day. Some of them are caused by the powers of nature; many are accidental; but may are due to the weaknesses of humanity, and they are violent. Those who experience a traumatic event can become mentally frozen in it, unable to function fully in the present. They have Post-Traumatic Stress Disorder [PTSD]. Awareness of the inner self becomes restricted. Access to the spirit is blocked by an ongoing obsession with the past and by energy-consuming efforts to cope with the anguish.

The expressive direction of the person with PTSD is determined largely by the emotional nucleus of the disorder. Unfortunately, its principal component is rage. While working in areas of human-induced devastation, I have been struck by the prevalence of people filled with rage and ready to act on it. The intensity of the emotion, and even its origin, can be largely unconscious. Behavioral manifestations, therefore, are frequently irrational releases of this overwhelming rage or heated overreactions to situations that are understandably somewhat annoying. Criminal and terrorist organizations seek the services of PTSD victims, some of which are eager recruits.

Interestingly, many of the afflicted have not personally experienced the traumatic event that seems to control them, having inherited their PTSD syndrome from those who did. They are influenced by something which they cannot identify or understand, and they act on it by instinct.

I am speaking here of the cause-effect relationship of traumatic suffering and violence. It comes from many sources and directions. Often it is unrelieved, and as the incidence of unrelieved PTSD in the world expands, war becomes more likely. Everyone is in danger, and solutions must be found.

There is hope. I have witnessed miracles of healing during my work with PTSD patients – in Kosovo, Rwanda, and the Democratic Republic of the Congo; with the Zulu nation of South Africa ; and with American veterans of war. From the moment of healing, there would begin a life-changing alteration of personality. For example, men who had intimidated their spouse and children for years turned into gentle, nurturing members of the family. A man who longed for former days of guerilla warfare became a worker for peace. And people who had been despised and avoided for being consistently nasty would eventually earn positive comments from their critics. The treatment and healing did not inject love into these people. The loving spirit was there all along, obscured by the present stress of past events.

Having observed countless cases of such healing, I was convinced that God would bring lasting peace to many areas of unrest once He found enough healers that He could use to get the job done. I realized my preferred, precise method [Callahan's Thought Field Therapy diagnostics] couldn't reach the multitudes with a one-on one treatment format. I hoped someone might emerge who could organize and develop such a program that would relieve trauma on a very large scale.

Gunilla Hamne contacted me in 2006 and soon we were working together in Rwanda, treating survivors of the 1994 genocide. Some Rwandans, concealed in places of hiding, actually witnessed the machete murders of their families and friends. Those who lived, including ones who had been chopped and left for dead, have suffered immensely with survivor guilt. Obviously, the core problem of this population is a poignantly sensitive matter. For a counselor to be trusted and permitted to intervene, a delicately careful approach that reveals sincere compassion is an absolute necessity. Gunilla Hamne, who does care greatly, was able to earn the peoples' trust. My communications with Ulf Sandstrom convince me that he also cares deeply. Gunilla and Ulf are both driven and they share a vision. Their intentions are wonderful and their integrity is beyond question.

Gunilla and I treated Rwandan survivors individually with advanced Thought Field Therapy. As the first 150 individuals reached their goals of healing, all treatment sequences that had been necessary were recorded, then analyzed and positioned into a rather long treatment algorithm written for that patient population. That algorithm was very successful in Rwanda, and it even had success in neighboring African countries.

TTT has been designed differently, in response to pragmatic requirements. Given the large numbers of technicians needed to reach the masses of traumatized people, it was necessary to select a treatment that would be easy to remember and administer by these workers, many of whom are children. And, as you are about to discover in this book, things have been going very well for TTT. I think you will enjoy this book and hopefully join me in applauding Gunilla Hamne and Ulf Sandstrom for their efforts to provide wide-scale relief. There is a solid superstructure here, and I believe it will be able to support an evolving and effective program for finding peace on earth.

Altruism is abundance: abundance has no boundaries. Salute to the discoverers of Trauma Tapping Technique.

Dr Rajni and Dr Bhaskar Vyas
Gynecologist and surgeon, stem cell researchers, hypnotherapists, India

***

This book is a must read for everyone who has compassion for people in unstable conditions resulting from man-made and natural disaster. It is generated from many years of pragmatic experience in this thematic area which our traumatized world needs today. This toolkit is versatile, easy to use, and down to earth. It can be used by peace practitioners, religious leaders, local state and non state actors alike. In my capacity as a Peace Maker I find the techniques in this book impactful and transformative.

Pastor Dr. James Movel Wuye
Co Executive Director, Interfaith Mediation Centre, Nigeria

***

Inner injury is frequently a sustaining factor in conflict. This book is therefore important reading not only for those working in trauma relief, but also for those working in conflict transformation.

Dr Alan Channer
Documentary film maker specializing in peace-building and reconciliation, UK/Kenya

***

The most remarkable features of the material presented in Resolving Yesterday are the ease by which the Trauma Tapping Technique (TTT) can be taught and learned and its power to heal. This book is replete with moving examples of individuals healing themselves from horrific events from their past. It is inspiring to read how Hamne and Sandstrom, using TTT, bring healing to different areas that were devastated by war and cruelty. They also describe this method being applied to large groups, making it an efficient, culturally neutral and language independent tool. This book is a gift to the world, it should be read and applied wherever there is suffering.

Ronald Ruden MD, PhD
Creator of Havening Techniques, USA

* * *

This book is truly interesting. The language transfers human warmth. The content is down to earth and at the same time highly professional. From my own experience as a social pedagogue using TTT, I know the calm atmosphere that appears after a TTT session when people find peace of mind. Therefore it is meaningful and important to encourage the spreading of this method.

Andrea Slotte-Wikström
Social Pedagogue, Finland

* * *

UMUHUZA is an organization working for peaceful and healthy communities in Rwanda. In this work the TTT has played a big role, especially in the personal and collective trauma healing. Now the goal is reached: families are united and parents work together for a better future of their children. Read this book, learn and implement TTT in your community.

Didacienne Mukahabeshimana
Co-founder and President of UMUHUZA organization, Rwanda

* * *

We have seen that healing is possible with TTT. This has been confirmed by women and youth who's hearts were broken by the suffering of the genocide. I can cite those who have found self-confidence, inner peace and light, cure for headache and stomach pain. Those who had lost the meaning to live, those who have learned to love again. Thank you to Peaceful Heart Network for having supported the prevention and alleviation of the effects of violence.

Mukasarasi Godelieve
Coordinator SEVOTA, Rwanda

Gisenyi acrobats in Rwanda are street kids trained by volunteers in acrobatics and TTT.

The Components of This Book

This book has four components

1. The techniques
   – how you can use TTT and the related techniques for yourself and others

2. The stories of survivors
   – to inspire you and help you understand what results to expect

3. Ways of spreading the technique through multiplication
   – to show you how to start your own TTT peace projects at little or no cost

4. The underlying mechanisms of emotional and post-traumatic stress
   – to make it easier to understand how simply, yet effectively they can be handled

You will find different voices in this book. We, the main authors, Gunilla Hamne and Ulf Sandström, are working with the goal of spreading TTT to as many as possible. The purpose is to enable the future handling of emotional and post-traumatic stress with the same unquestionable simplicity that mouth to mouth resuscitation is administered at a drowning incident; a first aid method for anybody who is drowning in emotional stress.

Most of the text is written as "we". At times one of us will share a personal experience with the voice of "I". We have first-hand experience of using these methods for our own emotional issues, as well as working, teaching, and training others since 2007 in Rwanda, Congo, Chad, Uganda, Sierra Leone, South Sudan and Kenya as well as Sweden, Finland, India, USA and Canada.

Women from a reconciliation group workshop in Rilima, Rwanda.

WHAT IS TTT?

Participants at a workshop in New Delhi, India, at the 9th National Conference on Hypnotherapy.

First Aid for Emotional and Traumatic Stress

This book is about dealing with emotional and traumatic stress on an individual level, on a family and community level and finally, on a national and global level.

What counts as emotional and traumatic stress?

One person's pain can never be fully understood by another. In our work, we meet children who have seen their parents die violently in front of them. Children, who have been sexually and emotionally abused, who have been robbed of their integrity, their childhood and education. We meet young mothers who have been raped and bear children of rape whom they cannot attach to.

Experiences of this sort can create an invisible prison of the mind that forces a person to relive the emotional reactions every night as nightmares and flashbacks, every day in the form of fear, anxiety attacks or aggression.

However easy it may be to understand the stress created through traumas of this magnitude, there is emotional stress just as dangerous to our mental and physical health existing in the everyday life of many people living in parts of the world where there is peace and material wealth. There is trauma in being misunderstood or bullied, being different or unloved even in the best of situations.

Stress will also affect our immune system, and in the long run, it is believed to open the door to physical diseases, such as cancer and heart problems.

The Trauma Tapping Technique and the other methods described in this book are just as useful for milder forms of emotional distress.

Are You Sure it Is Traumatic Stress?

Many people in the areas of conflict or post-conflict don't know that they are traumatized. We sometimes say that a fish may not be able to explain water, may not even be aware of it.

Our colleague Robert Ntabwoba shares his experience of this.
"*I was born in a family from the Tutsi ethnic group, and if you know about Rwanda and what happened during the 100 days of genocide, starting in April 1994, you can imagine what a horrible period it was. I was 11 years old and trust me, I know how hard it can be to live a normal life after surviving a tragedy of this kind.*

I hid in the bushes and spent several nights and days alone in the rain with no food and being close to the killers in a big ditch. I was able to escape the killers, but it wasn't easy to notice that all those moments and what I had seen changed and affected my life.

At the end of 1994 the genocide was over officially, but many of us continued to live in memories of that unpleasant time for years to come. Everything I had seen was manifesting into nightmares as if it was happening again and again, and for me it seemed normal even though it was scary.

Before being treated and learning how to help others using the Trauma Tapping Technique, every night was as if the genocide was still happening. You can imagine how my days were affected, they were unhappy days most of them.

Healing is possible but only when you allow yourself to be treated. I didn't know I was traumatized. I thought having all those problems was who I had become after living through the genocide. I was insecure, had nightmares and got angry without reason. I thought: 'That is how life is.' I had no idea that it was a kind of sickness I was suffering from. Now I know, because after getting treated and learning the Trauma Tapping I feel completely different."

Sometimes people need examples of symptoms, to be able to understand that they can be symptoms of post-traumatic stress. During a TTT training in the community of Mumosho in eastern Congo we started talking about the symptoms of trauma, listing them on the blackboard in the classroom, for example problems sleeping, loss of hope, acting crazy or feeling aggressive.

The participants exclaimed:

"Maybe that's why Mama Rose is behaving so strangely, she is running around without clothes. She is actually traumatized."

"Aha, that's why I sleep so badly."

"So that's why my neighbor's children scream at night."

Somebody even said:

"Is that me you are writing about? I have all those symptoms."

We do not measure traumatic stress or make a diagnosis apart from the SUD scale of calibration, because in our context we don't find it necessary. Our definition of traumatic stress is when an emotionally charged memory or reaction from the past keeps coming to your mind in situations you cannot control, and makes you feel distressed in various ways. If it does, TTT can help alleviate that distress and the negative emotions and reactions connected to it.

We can never say one trauma is "bigger" than the other. We feel that it is not possible to measure suffering or pain other than subjectively.

These are some symptoms of emotional and post-traumatic stress (see more on page 133):

- Nightmares or difficulty sleeping
- Flashbacks
- Anxiety
- Fear/Anger/Irritation
- Feeling of revenge
- Headache
- Palpitation (heartbeat)
- Difficulty breathing
- Tension in muscles
- Digestion problems
- Substance abuse
- Instability
- Forgetfulness
- Difficulty trusting anybody
- Dissociation from body
- Hypertension
- Feeling weak
- Feeling worthless
- Being in a "bubble"
- Difficult to concentrate
- Feeling isolated
- Not able to think about the future
- Reliving the past constantly
- Thoughts of suicide

The Bottom Line

Do you feel emotionally uncomfortable? Connect to that uncomfortable emotion and use Trauma Tapping.

Marhonyi Namegabe in Mumosho, Congo, uses TTT in her school and community.

The Evolution of TTT

The effects of sensory treatment in the form of tapping was first documented by Dr Roger Callahan, who was combining his knowledge as a clinical psychologist with acupuncture and kinesiology while trying to find a treatment for water phobia in a woman called Mary. Mary was the first person to be treated successfully with tapping. Thirty years later she appeared in the Ophrah Winfrey show testifying that she was still free from her phobia.

When Roger Callahan started to research this more systematically he created a complete system combining tapping acupoints with muscle testing to treat emotional stress, phobias and other symptoms . He called the treatment Thought Field Therapy (TFT).

One of Dr Callahans students, Gary Craig, who had an engineering background, simplified TFT to make it every man's tool. The main simplification was to tap all the acupoints used in TFT, instead of trying to find out which ones might be involved in a specific issue. Gary Craig's version is called Emotional Freedom Techniques (EFT). Since then more than 30 different versions of tapping have been named.

Another of Dr. Callahan's students, Dr. Carl Johnson, was dedicated to help his colleagues in the US Marine Corps when they came back from the Vietnam War with stress symptoms. He focused specifically on the area of post-traumatic stress. During Dr. Carl Johnsons work in Kosovo he found TFT to provide incredible results with survivors of the conflict.

When Gunilla Hamne and Carl Johnson met in Rwanda to teach and treat orphans in 2007 he was using muscle testing, which is the original method from kinesiology used by Dr. Roger Callahan, to detect what combination of points were needed to be treated for different problems. He was also using the eye movements called 9 point gamut (see Brain Balancing).

The muscle testing was hard to teach and the eye movements of the 9 point gamut were considered weird by some and uncomfortable by others. These challenges made Gunilla Hamne simplify the procedure and develop the version that is now called TTT by skipping the muscle testing, using the same points for every person and exchanging the eye movements for two deep breaths. The results were very positive and the method practical to use, teach and multiply.

With TTT we don't use set-up phrases or affirmations, partly because they can be re-traumatizing and because many people find it very comfortable dealing with their traumatic experiences silently and internally, leaving out the verbal expression of words and concentrating instead on the process inwardly.

And as mentioned before: not using words means also not having to mention what one has lived through, be it connected to shame, guilt or sensitive information that one would rather keep inside, especially when working with groups. If you are doing TTT in groups we recommend the Somatic Poem as a setup to connect with the emotions instead.

We have simplified the Trauma Tapping Technique further, making it transferable and content free so that large groups of people can experience the benefits without the need for personal questions, abreactions or spoken words. This is especially useful and important when constrained by language barriers which can largely be skirted by this approach and make TTT eminently practical.

We consider the key components of TTT in the way we teach and spread it to be:
- Content free
- Replicable by anyone
- A First Aid
- Simple to remember
- Empowering
- Language free to 99%
- Efficient and powerful enough to bring peace to individuals and society
- Easy to combine with other therapies or treatments
- Works great with music and dance
- Simple to multiply

Why these points?

When applying TTT we stimulate 14 specific points on the upper part of the body. The same points are used in similar psycho-sensory treatments such as

TFT and EFT. Why are these points used?

Any touch on the skin creates sensory input and generates electrochemical signals in the body that will be registered by the brain, activating the autonomous nervous system, triggering responses and production of hormones and neurochemicals.

Some points of the body are more sensitive and register more information than other; you can compare tapping under the eye with tapping on your knee to get a general idea. The points used in TTT correlate with points used in traditional Chinese medicine which dates back over 5 000 years in treatments like acupuncture, acupressure and shiatsu.

It is likely that other points could be used, however, we know from experience that the points used in TTT are both highly functional and easy to remember, therefore, we stick to them.

Why Two Rounds?

A TTT session is complete only after doing the tapping sequence twice.

Our experience shows that change starts during the first round of tapping. The breathing between the rounds also calms down the nervous system. The second round of tapping often moves emotions, images or symptoms further away, or dissolves them completely.

Washing Needs Rinsing

During the genocide in Rwanda, first and foremost men and boys were killed, since they were presumed to become soldiers and fight back. Due to this at lot of our workshops in Rwanda are done for the widows of the genocide.

At one time we were conducting a workshop in the shadow of a big mango tree next to the school in a village called Ngororero, high up on one of the thousand hills of Rwanda. Everybody was sitting on the ground, and people gathered to see what was going on. Some were laughing and pointing at us, commenting about the tapping gestures. A group of children in school uniforms were giggling.

When we had gone through the procedure a couple of times, one of the widows asked: *"Why should we do the tapping protocol twice? Seems unnecessary doing the same thing again."*

Our colleague Robert Ntabwoba answered: "*You know, when you are washing clothes, first you put them in water with soap and shrug them, don't you?*"

The women nodded their heads, confirming what he had said.

"*That is the first round of tapping, ok? Then you take out the clothes from the soapy water and wring them. The wringing is like the breathing between the tappings. Then you get clean water in your bucket and rinse the clothes, don't you?*"

The women nodded affirmatively again.

"*That is the second round of tapping. And again you wring and hang the clothes in the sun, right?*"

"But" he added, "*if you see that there are still some spots of dirt on your clothes, when you have hung them on the line, you will then wash again, won't you? That is exactly the same with the tapping: If, after the two rounds of tapping, you find that you still feel some discomfort, then you continue by doing another round of tapping.*"

Laughter and applause. Washing and rinsing. That's TTT.

Presenting Trauma Tapping

There are different ways of presenting TTT depending the context of the situation. We often divide the presentation into three categories:

1. A relaxation method for all types of stress
If you are working in school, with elderly, with refugees or at a similar workplace, you can present TTT as a relaxation method for all types of stress, also over language barriers. Most people using TTT will feel relaxed after a session even if it is done in groups, applied on their own or by somebody, and without the context of therapy. In this context we don't even mention the word "therapy" or discuss the reasons for stress. We present TTT as a relaxation method – we offer people to try it to feel calmer.

2. An additional tool to other forms of therapy or body treatments
If you are a counselor, psychotherapist, coach, massage or for example shiatsu therapist, TTT is an efficient complementary tool. You can present it as a way to relax emotionally challenging thoughts and memories if and when they appear, and then continue with your main method of change.

3. A therapeutic intervention for stress and trauma
TTT is a powerful therapeutic tool of its own. A single session can release long kept emotionally charged memories of the past, whether they are consciously remembered, felt in the body as a pain or discomfort or an undefined unpleasant feeling in general. Follow the instructions in the first chapter to apply as a therapeutic tool.

A Little Bird

This is the story about Gazelle who cannot sleep and talks about it with Zebra at the waterhole, told in the tradition of African storytelling.

Gazelle wonders if she is sleepless because she's living in constant fear of Crocodile. Zebra knows the feeling, but has his own problems, those of nightmares and flashbacks from being chased by Lion.

Both Gazelle and Zebra are very tired. Although neither Lion nor Crocodile have been seen in this valley for months, they are living in constant anticipation, jumping at small noises and yelling at their offspring for little reason.

In this valley there is a small bird that picks the teeth of Crocodile when he sleeps with his mouth open in the sun. "*Imagine...*", said Gazelle to Zebra, "*Imagine if a bird like that could come and pick our worries out of our heads and bodies as we speak...*"

The little bird heard them and landed on the head of Zebra. "*How can I be of help?*" it asked.

"*We are both so very tired and we don't know why, because there is no danger at this moment like there was a while back*", answered Zebra.

The little bird flew high up in the air, so high that it could see the calm of the water, the green of the grass, and the energy of life in Zebra... and this energy was like small rivers of pure life flowing from the hooves to the head to the heart and around... but some of these rivers did not seem to flow properly, as if they were dried up or blocked.

That night, as Zebra looked into the stars, the little bird started tapping with its beak, firmly but gently, to awaken the rivers of life under the eyes of Zebra... at the side of the head... over the lips, under the lips... the little bird was like a drummer drumming for life to come back.

At one point Zebra took two really deep breaths and suddenly felt like a blanket was lifted, like getting air after being closed into a cave, like finding light after darkness...

"*What did you do little bird?*" Zebra asked. But the little bird had flown away... Zebra tried to explain to Gazelle what happened, but to Gazelle it sounds like a fairytale, how silly it seemed...

That night when Gazelle tried to sleep, Zebra took the very tip of the hoof and tapped ever so gently but firmly on the same healing points around the eyes, lips, chest and hooves of Gazelle, and the reaction was different... Gazelle went from irritated, to crying, to shivering, to sleep... with a smile that only the sun could compete with... And as the little bird knows and the river of life can tell, healing is possible and can be passed on...

A bird outside our guesthouse in Kigali, Rwanda.

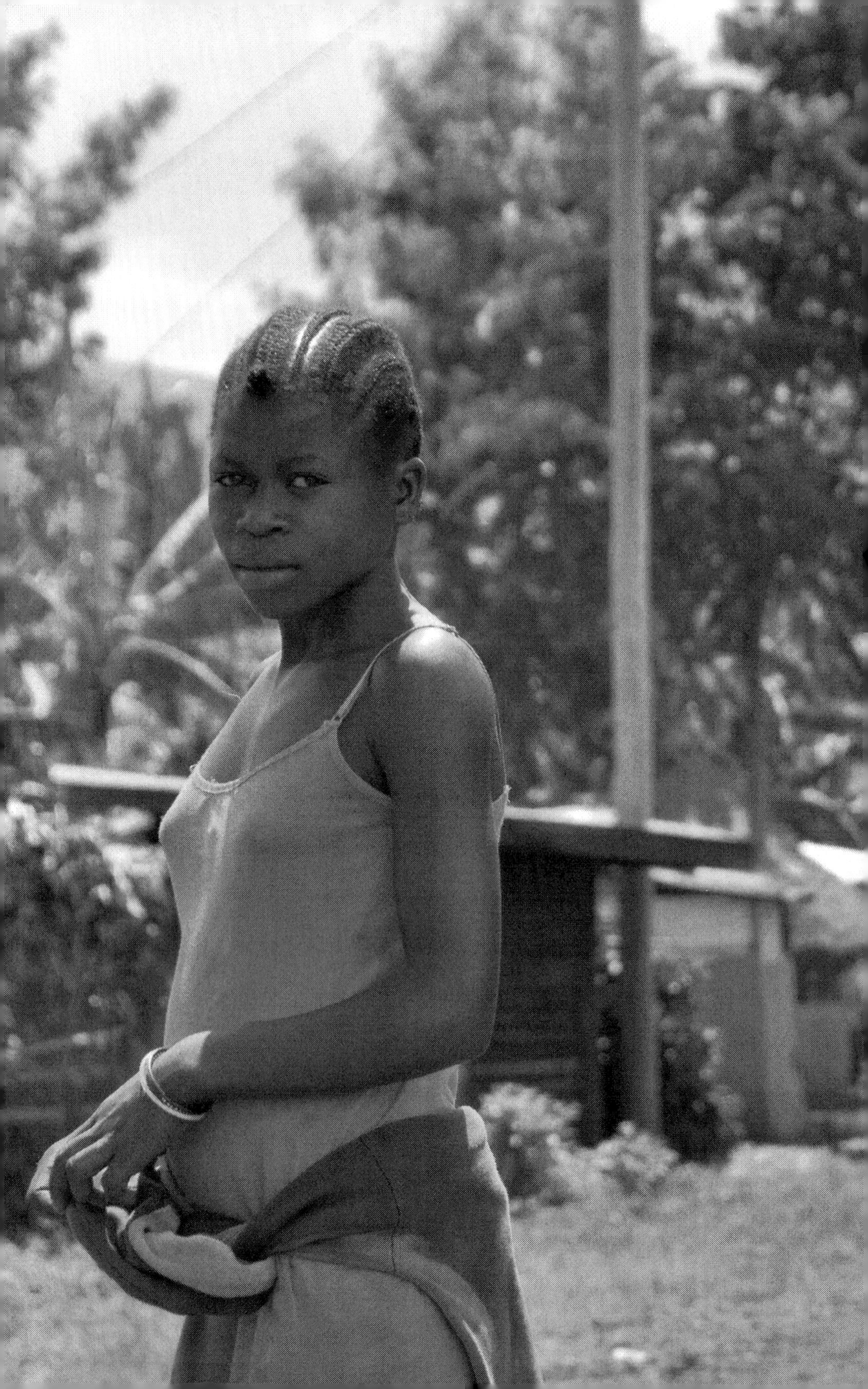

SELF HELP WITH TTT

The road through Musanze below the Virunga Mountains in Rwanda.

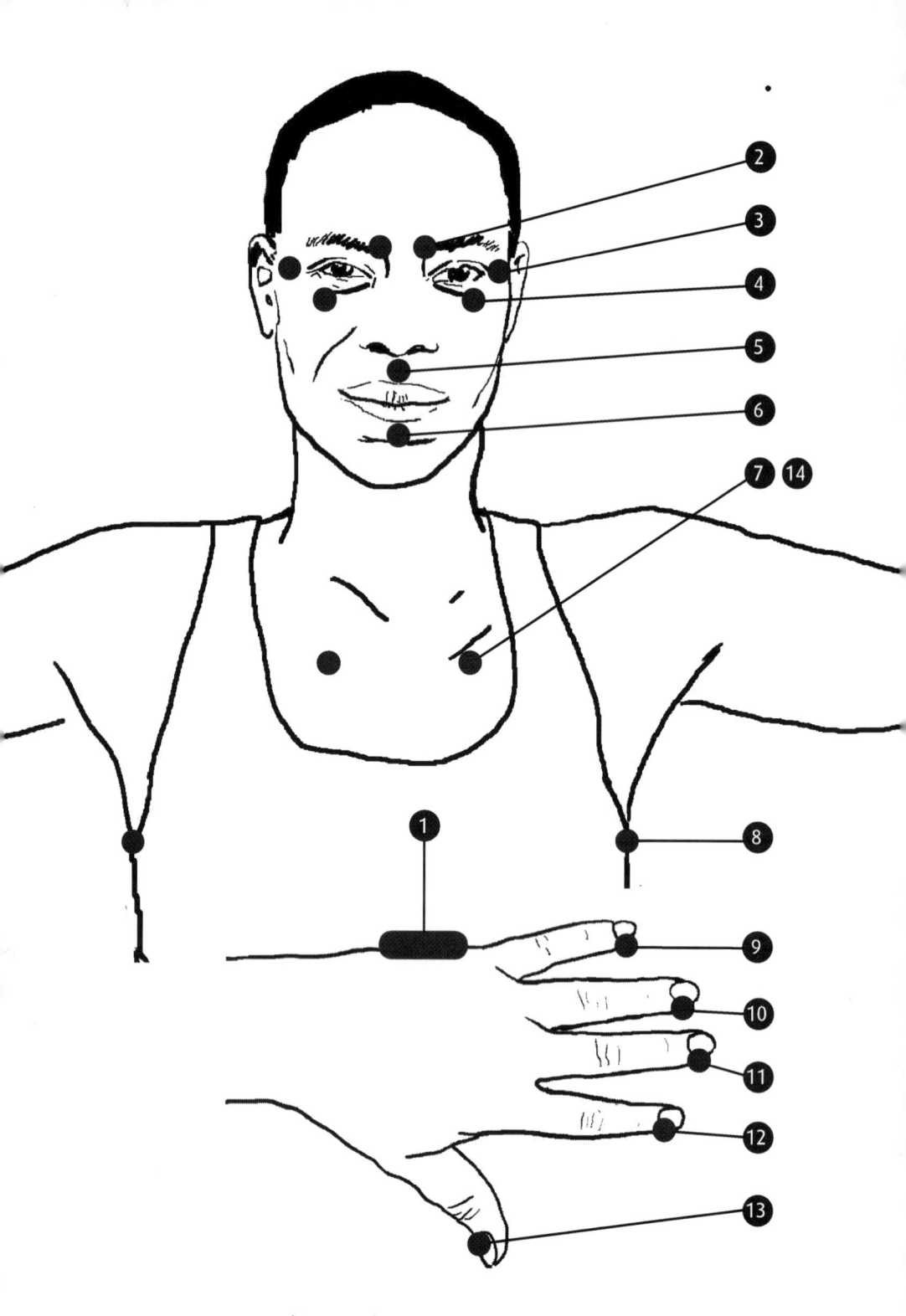

Resolving Yesterday - First Aid for Stress and Trauma with TTT

The Trauma Tapping Technique (TTT)

This is how Trauma Tapping is done. There is more to it, but we want you to know the basic technique before you read further. You can apply this technique to yourself or to somebody else.

1. Connect to the emotion that bothers you, ever so slightly
2. Tap 15 times, firmly but gently – on the points in the picture below
3. Take two deep breaths – short in and long out
4. Repeat the tapping procedure as described above
5. Take two deep breaths – short in and long out
6. Relax and breathe normally
7. When treating somebody else finish by holding their hand between yours and wait for them to be ready

Points
1. Side of the hand ("Karate Point")
2. Beginning of the eyebrow
3. Outside the eye on the bone
4. Under the eye
5. Under the nose
6. Under the mouth
7. Under the collarbone on the chest
8. Under the arm, on the side of the chest
9. The inside tip of the little finger
10. The inside tip of the ring finger
11. The inside tip of the middle finger
12. The inside tip of the index finger
13. The outside tip of the thumb
14. Under the collarbone and on the whole chest, like drumming

Self Tapping Step by Step

Think about whatever bothers you, and tap firmly and precisely 15 times on each point using two fingers, at a fairly fast rate. Take two deep breaths and repeat the whole sequence twice. Take two deep breaths again when done.

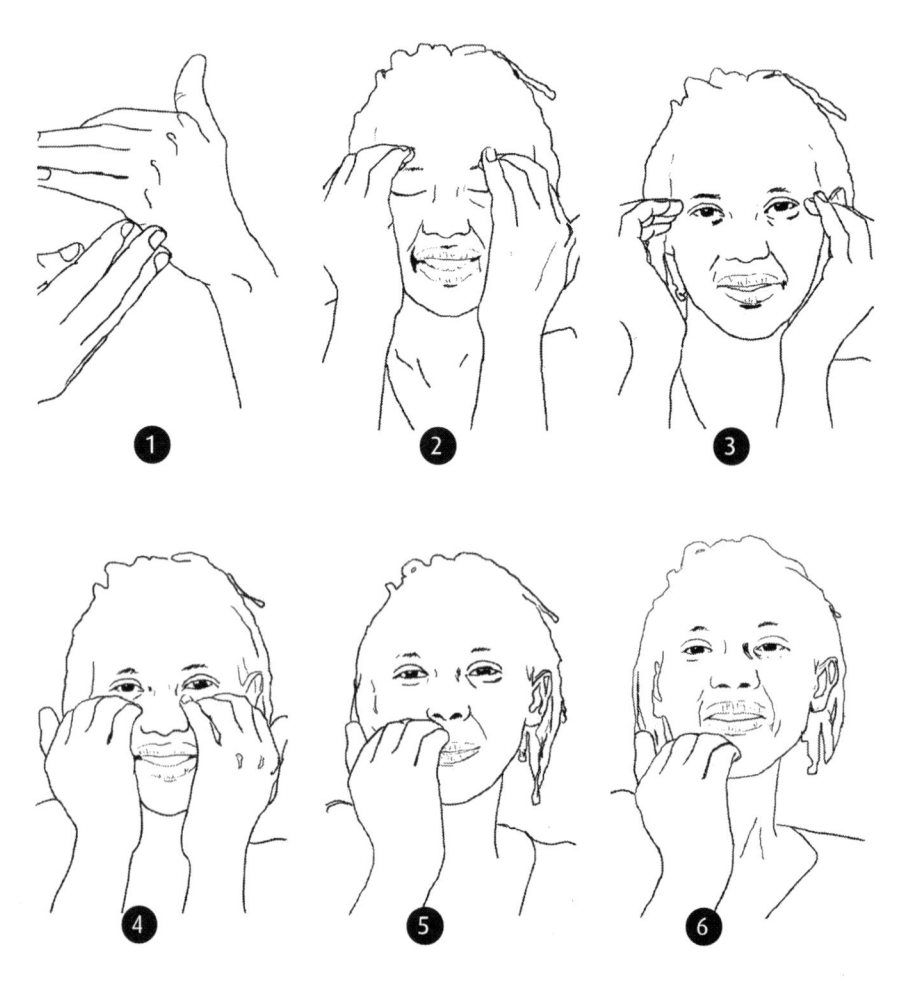

Resolving Yesterday - First Aid for Stress and Trauma with TTT

Take two deep breaths

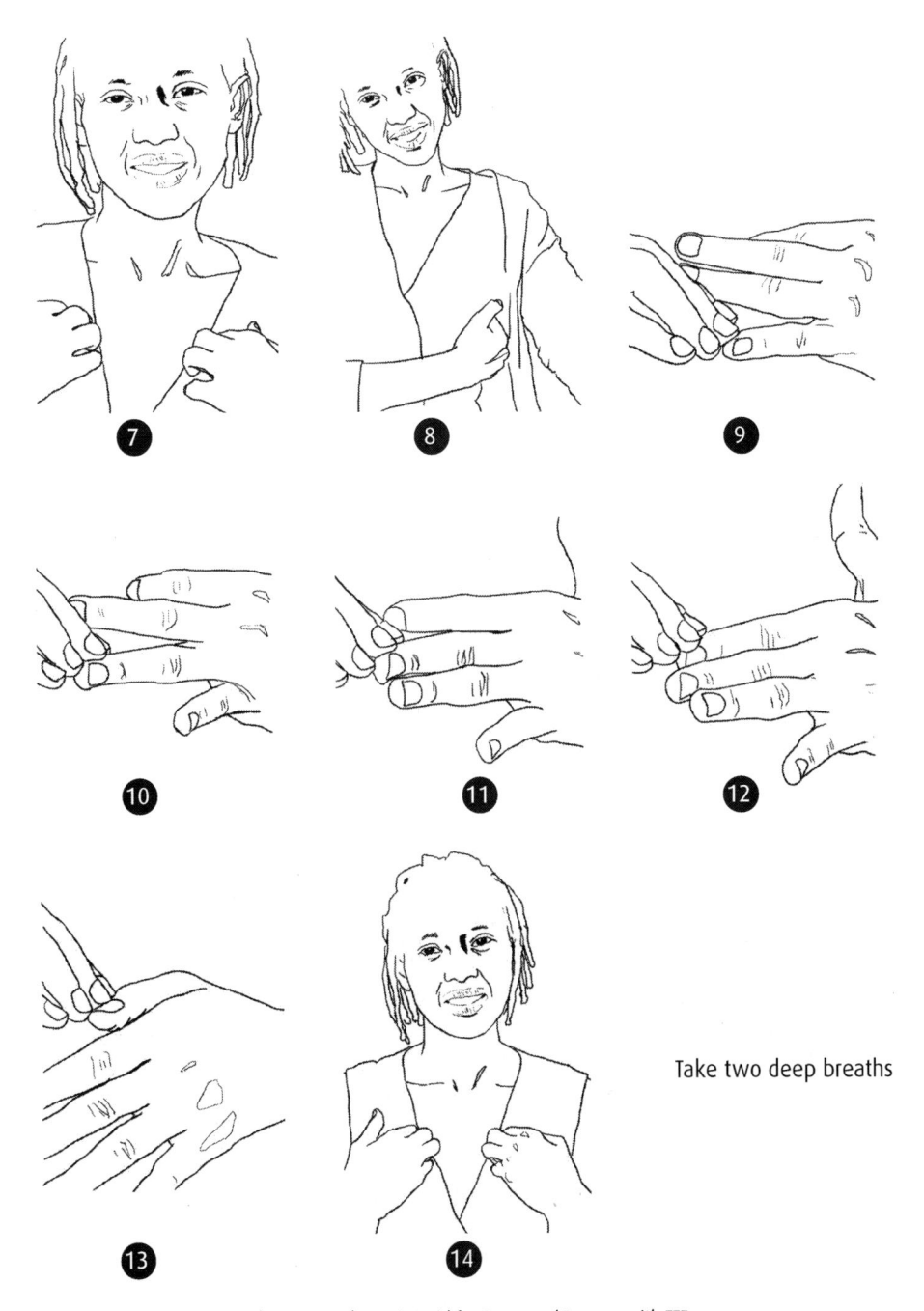

Resolving Yesterday - First Aid for Stress and Trauma with TTT

A workshop in Cyuve, Rwanda, close to the border of Congo.

OFFERING A TTT SESSION

Training with Peace Mothers group of Fambul Tok in Sierra Leone.

Who Can Be Treated?

"Contrary to popular belief trauma can be healed, trauma is not a life sentence."

Dr. Peter Levine

All types of emotional and traumatic stress can be treated with TTT. This is our experience from years of working with the Trauma Tapping Technique in Rwanda, Congo, Senegal, Sierra Leone, Chad, Kenya, Uganda, South Sudan, India, Canada, Sweden, Denmark and Finland.

We have been working with the most vulnerable individuals of each society and professionals involved with these. Since 2007 when we started teaching tapping to orphans of the genocide in Rwanda together with trauma expert Dr. Carl Johnson, we have worked with victims of sexual violence and rape, survivors of war, refugees, former child soldiers, victims of torture, widows, and the families of these. These are survivors of some of the most unimaginable acts of violence and war, and they are unquestionably able to heal.

Before a Session

There are things you should consider before offering a session of TTT to somebody:

Healing Is Possible

In our experience it is possible to heal even from incredibly severe emotional trauma. However, healing may need to be defined: it is not about forgetting what happened to you. It is about being able to bring back memories of what happened, without triggering emotionally loaded responses that cause undue stress. Stress reactions from a traumatic event can endure over 15-20 years or more, and we acknowledge that it may seem preposterous to claim that this can be healed in a tapping session or two, but it is a fact in our world. We have personally have met thousands of survivors of genocide, war, slavery, mutilation, rape and violence, and witnessed their healing process. Our message is simple: Healing is possible.

Congruency, Confidence and Being Centered

Congruency and confidence in what you do and why you do it are the most important assets in working with emotional trauma using TTT or any other method. Without these assets treating or teaching will not proceed ahead.

It is also important to be present and focused on the wellbeing of the person you are assisting. A session is all about them. Being centered in yourself applies in all healing work, but also to life in general. Exercises like meditation, praying, qigong, mindfulness, and relaxation are helpful. We also recommend self-tapping and Do-in.

Stand, Sit or Lay Down
We treat and teach TTT both standing and sitting, and the technique works just as well for somebody who is laying down, especially somebody sick, giving birth or a child falling asleep. However, be careful if you are treating somebody who is deeply distressed while standing, because the relaxation effect of the treatment can give "weak knees".

Sit Down Like Two Ships Passing
If you are sitting, we recommend that you sit down with the chairs set like two ships passing each other. This position allows you to reach all points with ease without invading the personal space of the person being treated.

Explain Before and During
Always explain what you are about to do and show the points on yourself, to get an OK from the person you are about to treat to touch these points on them. If their eyes are closed during the session let them know when you move your hands by saying for example *"Now I am going to touch your forehead."* so they feel safe and can relax without being surprised at your touch. Learn the science of stress and trauma, as explained in Understanding Stress (page 53).

Eyes Open or Closed
It is fine for a person to receive the treatment with their eyes open, but there can be a greater effect if their eyes are closed, since it allows them to relax and focus on their internal sensations. Also, you can check the eyelids for fluttering, which is a good sign, of relaxation.

Be Humble
Never promise any specific results before a session. Every person is unique and sometimes the results of a session show up a day or a week later, depending on the stimulus required to trigger the stress reaction.

You could say:

"If you want to experience a method that may allow you to relax, I can show it to you."

"I know a method for relaxing emotional distress that can be useful even with severe traumatic experiences. I use it for myself at times, do you want me to show you?"

Agree to Continue until Peace

Emotions can rest on top of each other like layers of skin on an onion. If anxiety lets go during a session it can resolve into anger, then grief, then peace. If a strong emotion surfaces during a tapping-session, we recommend to keep tapping for another round focusing on the new emotion. If this happens it is good to get permission to continue before starting again.

Connect to the Emotion

For TTT to have an effect, the person being treated has to be connected to the emotion they wish to treat, which is why TTT works perfectly if applied during an emotional reaction. If they are not connected to the emotion they wish to treat the effect will be a slight relaxation, lowering of cortisol levels and peace of mind but the reaction can resurface.

We often say that doing TTT without connecting to the emotion you wish to treat, is like turning on a shower and never getting in.

Evaluate before and after

The evaluation before a session can be as simple as saying "*If you think about it now, on a scale from 1–10, where 0 is no distress and 10 is very much, how strong is your emotional response?*" This is referred to as a Subjective Units of Distress (SUD) scale.

Evaluating makes it easier for the other person and for you to notice what the difference is after the session.

Explain that TTT is a First Aid Method

Trauma Tapping is not always presented as a therapy. We often call it a first aid method for psychological or emotional distress, a relaxation method, or a self-help method for clearing the mind.

This way TTT becomes something every person is qualified to try, putting the power of healing in the hands of the individual. A trained practitioner will have more experience and may be able to get better results than a beginner, but in many situations a simple method like TTT is good enough to make a big difference.

Trust the Method

TTT is a generous method. We recommend it to be performed as described here, but if you happen to tap in a different order or forget some points, don't worry. Even if you don't do it exactly how it is described in the book, it usually brings change anyway. Nothing bad will happen that hasn't already happened for this person. Trust the method.

No Words Needed

For TTT to work it is only necessary to connect to the emotion involved, there is no need for verbal archeology into what may have caused it. There are many reasons why this might be of benefit:

1. Low-trust areas

In societies where rumors and information have been used for false accusations, trust is low and people may not want to say out loud what they lived through. For example, in Chad during the dictatorship of Hissein Habré in the 1990s the use of spies and informants was very widely spread and people got arrested and tortured.

During a workshop with victims of torture in N'Djamena, the capital of Chad, one of the participants commented:

"In that time, you could not even trust your own shadow. There were informants everywhere and some of them are still in power. Therefore there is no trust in our society. We appreciate this Trauma Tapping that allows us to deal with our memories without having to talk about our experiences."

2. Dealing with shame

When dealing with rape or harm done to others, as the case may be with children who have been forced into armed groups, most don't want to talk about it, because of the shame involved.

3. Privacy

Sometimes people prefer to keep their memories and history private for any other reason and simply don't want to talk about their problems with others.

4. Language barriers
A person can still be helped even though their story cannot be understood verbally, as long as they understand enough to accept a session and are connected to their emotion.

Speak positively
When a medically ineffectual treatment has a positive effect on a condition, there is a placebo effect. There is an element of placebo effect in every treatment, including TTT.

Every word you use will matter! Allow your client to keep and maintain any belief that supports them in healing. If people believe in a God, a spirit world or science: Leave their beliefs in peace, they are sources of energy.

Nocebo is the opposite of placebo; it is when words limit or stop the healing process. Imagine the effects of a doctor or a therapist saying:

"Trauma is severe and chronic. You will have to learn to live with it."

Now imagine the effect of the same person saying:

"I know of many cases of trauma similar to yours that have healed, and sometimes even faster than you would think possible."

It is also important to be honest. You cannot ask a person to feel good or positive if they don't. You cannot ask a person to accept themselves if they haven't yet.

A way of wording that we have found 100% honest and congruent for any person in any situation is:

"I wish to feel (good, calm, relaxed, happy) and I am willing to do everything in my power to do so."

This is a positive goal without illusions and with a clear intent.

Change Suffering to Joy
The most healing power of this world is laughter. Laughter is a natural reaction when you release tension and find a new perspective on your challenges. We use a lot of humor in our workshops, and we promote humor as one of the most important tools of healing. Cultivate your humor and practice smiling.

Treat - and even better: Teach!
Teach people more than you treat them. You can empower people by helping them realize that they have the ability to heal both themselves and others.

A Frequent Question

Many people think tapping looks ridiculous, like a joke. We often get the question *"Do I have to believe in TTT for this to work?"* The answer is no. Belief has nothing to do with it and even if there is a placebo effect in all treatments, TTT works on a neurological level beyond your belief system. The only requirement is that you are in touch with the feeling or emotion you wish to treat.

Treat the Whole Family

When a person is affected by traumatic stress, the response can be transferred to every member of the family. Teaching the technique to all family members, preferably at the same time, provides a tool empowering them to take control of the situation. It also breaks any existing barrier of trust or hierarchy since children can treat parents and vice versa.

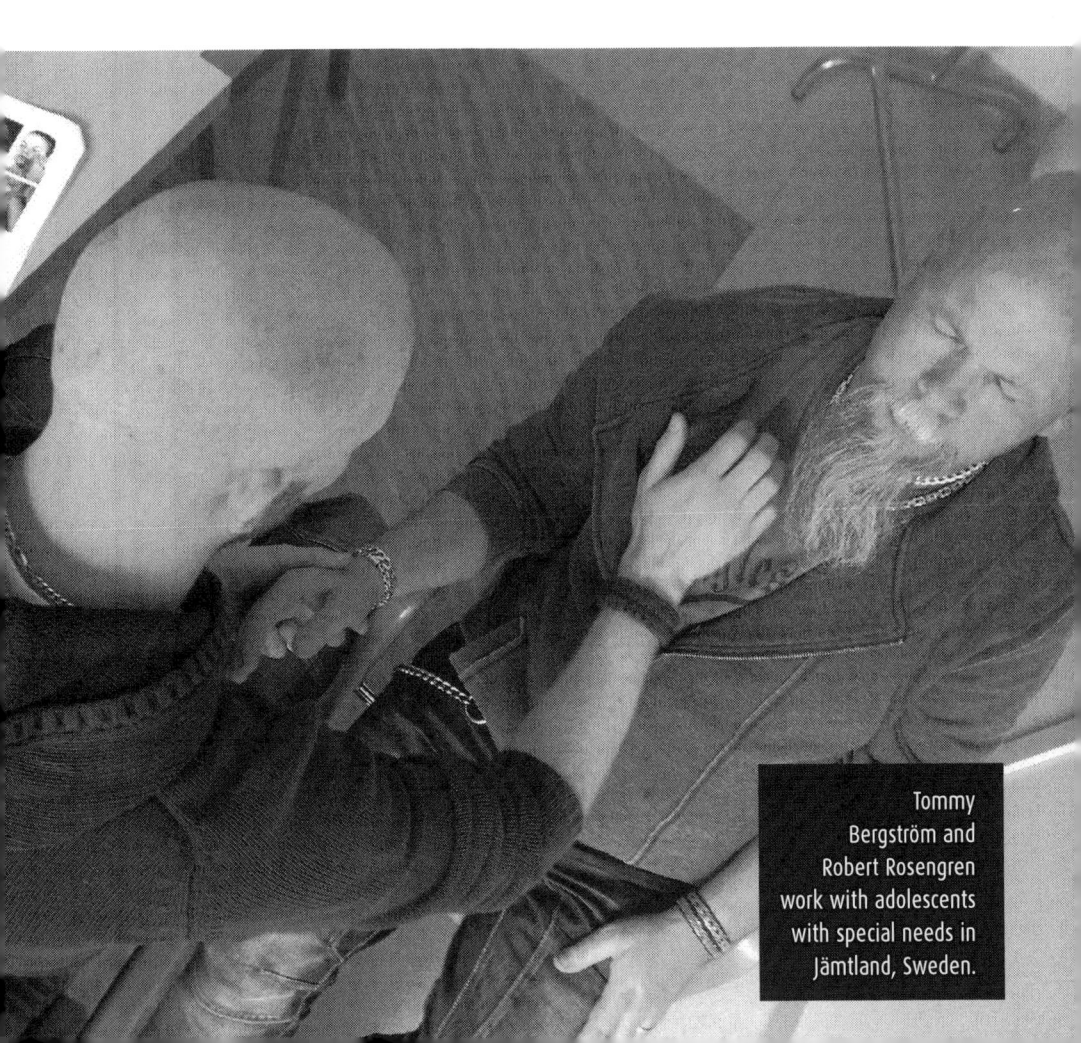

Tommy Bergström and Robert Rosengren work with adolescents with special needs in Jämtland, Sweden.

During A Session

You might want to consider the following during a session:

No Suffering!
A memory should never be revisited so deeply that the emotion becomes overwhelming.

After working with TTT in areas with deep traumas of war and genocide for many years, our experience is that every traumatic stress response can be healed when approached carefully and with common sense, never unnecessary flooding or reliving memories because of the risk for re-traumatization, reinforcing and making the symptoms worse.

If people being treated should start to flood with emotions, or show signs of panic, you can distract them by simply asking them to open their eyes, changing the subject or asking them to perform a simple math calculation, like 7+2, that forces them to use their rational mind.

> *"If you start suffering, please let me know and allow us to talk about something else, like the flowers in your garden, football or your favorite food. I don't want you to suffer. You have already suffered so much"*
>
> Dr. Carl Johnson during an early training in Rwanda

Firmly and Precisely
The tapping is done with two fingers, with the tips of the fingers. Perform it firmly and precisely. Not too soft and not too rough. Be gentle, calibrate, and adjust when necessary.

Long fingernails will be a bit difficult because you will not be able to achieve the same effect. Try to find a way around it or consider trimming your nails on two fingers.

Wash your hands before a session, not only for the obvious hygienic reasons, but also because the smell of something you have handled previously can be a negative distraction.

The Healing Of Touch

"Hold the hand of the patient!"

Hippocrates, physician and the father of Western medicine.

Many times people being treated with TTT will close their eyes Make sure to be in touch at all times: allow your fingers to trace on the skin from one point to the next on the face, it is reassuring and reinforces the process.

Between the two rounds of Trauma Tapping, during the deep breathing, and after the session we recommend you to hold the hand of the client between your hands, until he or she is ready to move on.

The Arm Drop

Every time you drop the hand or arm of the client, you may swing it gently right-left and drop it on their legs from a slight height. If the person is relaxed, the hand usually drops as if they are sleeping, sometimes it will stay in the air when you let go of it. Regardless of which, this will often have the effect of deepening the relaxation process.

The Hand Hold for Finger Tapping

When you get to points 9-13 on the tips of the fingers, it helps to put the fingers on the knee or a table. When you are treating somebody you can make a "left hand shake" that allows you to tap the fingers against your own hand or wrist.

Do I Treat Both Sides of the Body?

We have found that it doesn't matter if you treat both sides of the body or not. You can tap on one side during the first round and the other side on the second round, or the same side on both. The body seems to compensate for this.

Resolving Yesterday - First Aid for Stress and Trauma with TTT

After A Session

It is important to give the person some quiet time for recalibration and peace after a session.

You can ask them what the Subjective Units of Distress (SUD) level (0-10) of the emotion or feeling is after the tapping, when bringing back the same memories that they thought of in the pre-evaluation. In some situations, we just say "*What do you notice?*".

What can I expect?
There can be many positive effects of a TTT session
- Feeling relaxed
- Feeling sleepy
- Feeling energized
- Change of feelings
- New feelings bubbling up
- Laughter or tears
- Disconnecting pain from memories
- Feeling positively confused
- Feeling happy

Our experience is that every new emotion during or after a session is a sign of change going on. If a negative emotion surfaces in a TTT session there is a simple solution: do a second session on the new emotion. We guarantee that if you follow this instruction, the person will end up feeling relaxed. Feelings are layered like the skin of an onion. Grief can be followed by anger, followed by sorrow, then emptiness or laughter. Always make an agreement to continue until the person finds peace or calm.

Immediate Success

Many sessions produce an immediate and noticeable feeling of improvement in the emotional system of the person treated. We never take credit if there is a positive change, no matter how overwhelming. The person you treat needs to be empowered and to understand that you simply added some help from the outside and the healing was something they created on the inside. We usually end a session by congratulating the person.

Unclear Change

Sometimes people say "I don't know" when asked how they feel after a session. This is a good answer, because, if they are experiencing a new emotion, that isn't negative, they actually don't know what it means yet.

Allow every individual's healing process as much time as needed. Avoid jumping to conclusions that it did or didn't work. Some symptoms disappear right away whereas others may require a few days.

We tell the person to look for the slightest difference in feelings towards the memory that was activated during the tapping session. Even if the difference seems small, also the slightest ray of light that comes into a completely dark room will make it possible to see when the eyes have adjusted.

Allow for a night's sleep to process and suggest a new session the day after.

Less Common Reactions

After a session, the majority usually feel relaxed. At times there may be physical reactions such as

- Sleepiness
- Nausea
- Headache
- Sweating
- Shaking

These are signs that a change is going on. We always make an agreement to be allowed to continue with one more session if something like this arises.

Gunilla:
One of my friends in Sweden wanted a tapping for a traumatic experience that he was holding inside. He knows the procedure very well so I didn't have to ex-

plain anything. He sat down on a chair in the middle of his kitchen. He closed his eyes and prepared his mind on the issue he wanted to treat.

Afterward the tapping he first felt very relaxed but then he began sweating very strongly. He had to take a shower. The body releases things in different ways. Some, like my friend, find this natural. Others find it strange or uncomfortable. In our western society we have learned that pain, vomiting, fever and sweating are unwanted feelings and reactions.

Among traditional healers in the Amazon, and yogis in India, vomiting is considered a very important way of releasing tension and problems.

Feeling Empty

Traumatic emotions can take a lot of space. After a treatment where the symptoms of trauma are dissolved, some people feel empty, almost hollow. You can assist them by suggesting they fill this emptiness with something they prefer instead: light, calm, your true self, love. Breathe in whatever you would like to feel instead, and do a round of tapping on this positive feeling.

Does the effect of TTT last?

One very relevant question that we often get is: "*Does the effect of the Trauma Tapping Technique last?*"

A simple answer is: "*Yes, forever.*"

This may sound bold and naive, but our experience proves it true. Many of the orphans we trained in the first sessions in Rwanda had seen their parents and siblings killed in front of their eyes, they had been covered by dead bodies in a church, witnessed murder as they were hiding in a ceiling, in a sorghum field or in the papyrus swamps. They had been in hiding, surrounded by barking dogs and burning houses.

Some of them survived by eating raw cassava and other roots or leaves, while their friends or family died from starvation and pneumonia, others were caught in road blocks and killed on the spot.

The symptoms we treated have been gone during the 7 years we have known them. The memories are there, but not with the devastating emotional charge they carried before applying TTT.

A more complex answer is: "*Yes, if all the emotions involved, or a critical mass of them, were exposed at the time of the TTT treatment, the effect is likely to last forever.*"

Theoretically, you can apply TTT to any person and induce a relaxed state of mind, lower the stress levels and create a temporary relief. When a person goes back to the environment where the traumatic experience happened, some symptoms can be triggered that were never treated. A person who has learned TTT can treat themselves.

A dancer from our Tapping song video shoot in Rwanda.

Workshop with Batwa pygmies in Buyungule in eastern Congo.

Now Try!

"I've never made a mistake. I've only learned from experience."

Thomas Edison

If you have read this far and haven't tried a tapping session yet, you are more than ready now.

It is the same with all practical techniques: you can read about them and think intellectually that it may or may not work, and then put this knowledge in your large internal library of "things to be tried at some point" and move on – or you can convert it into a real experience and know for real.

If you are on your own, find a calm place and put the instructions with the tapping points in front of you, connect to the unwanted emotion and tap yourself.

If you want to treat somebody, sit down like two ships passing as described in the section "Before a Session" and put the instructions so you can see the points, ask the other person to connect to the emotion and tap the two rounds.

There are instruction videos on our website: www.peacefulheart.se

Tapping Somebody Step by Step

Connect to the emotion, then tap firmly and precisely 15 times on each point using two fingers, at a fairly fast rate. Take two deep breaths and repeat.

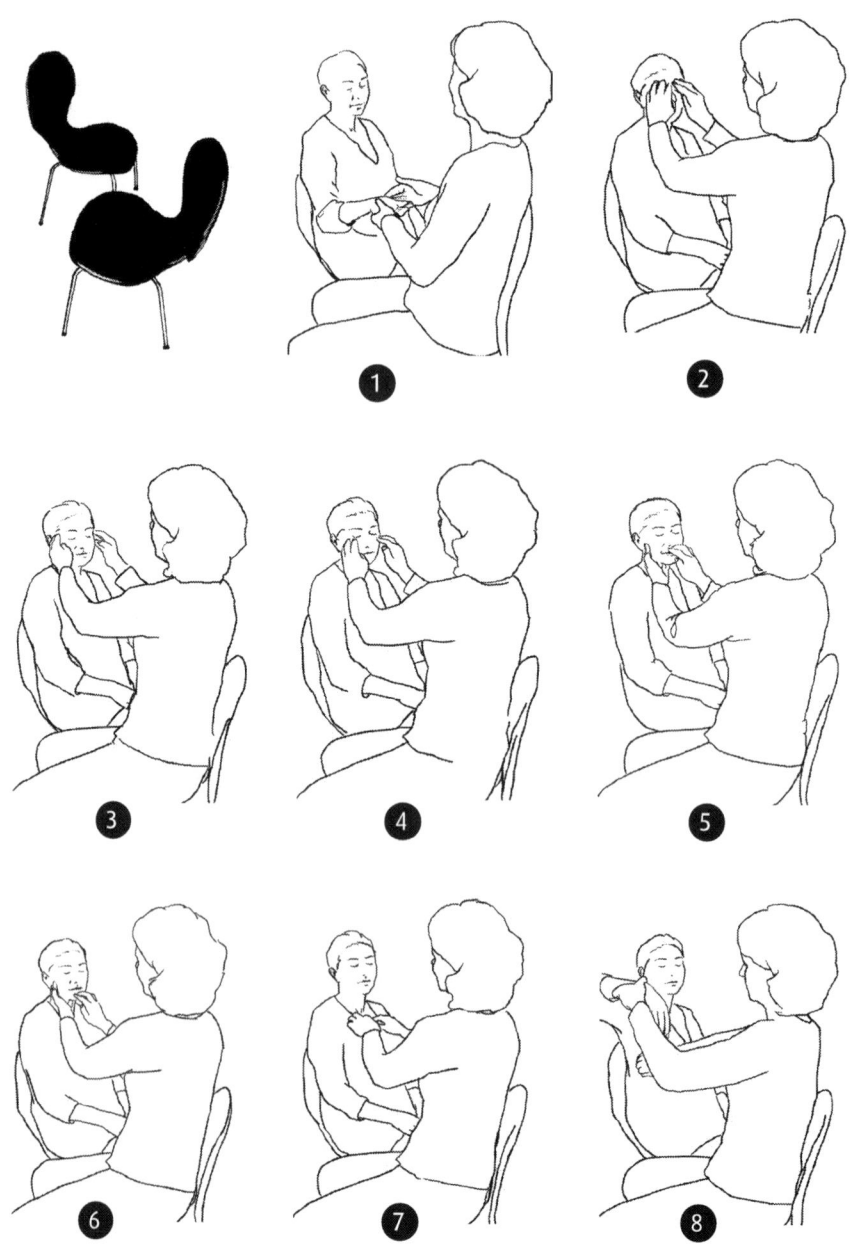

Resolving Yesterday - First Aid for Stress and Trauma with TTT

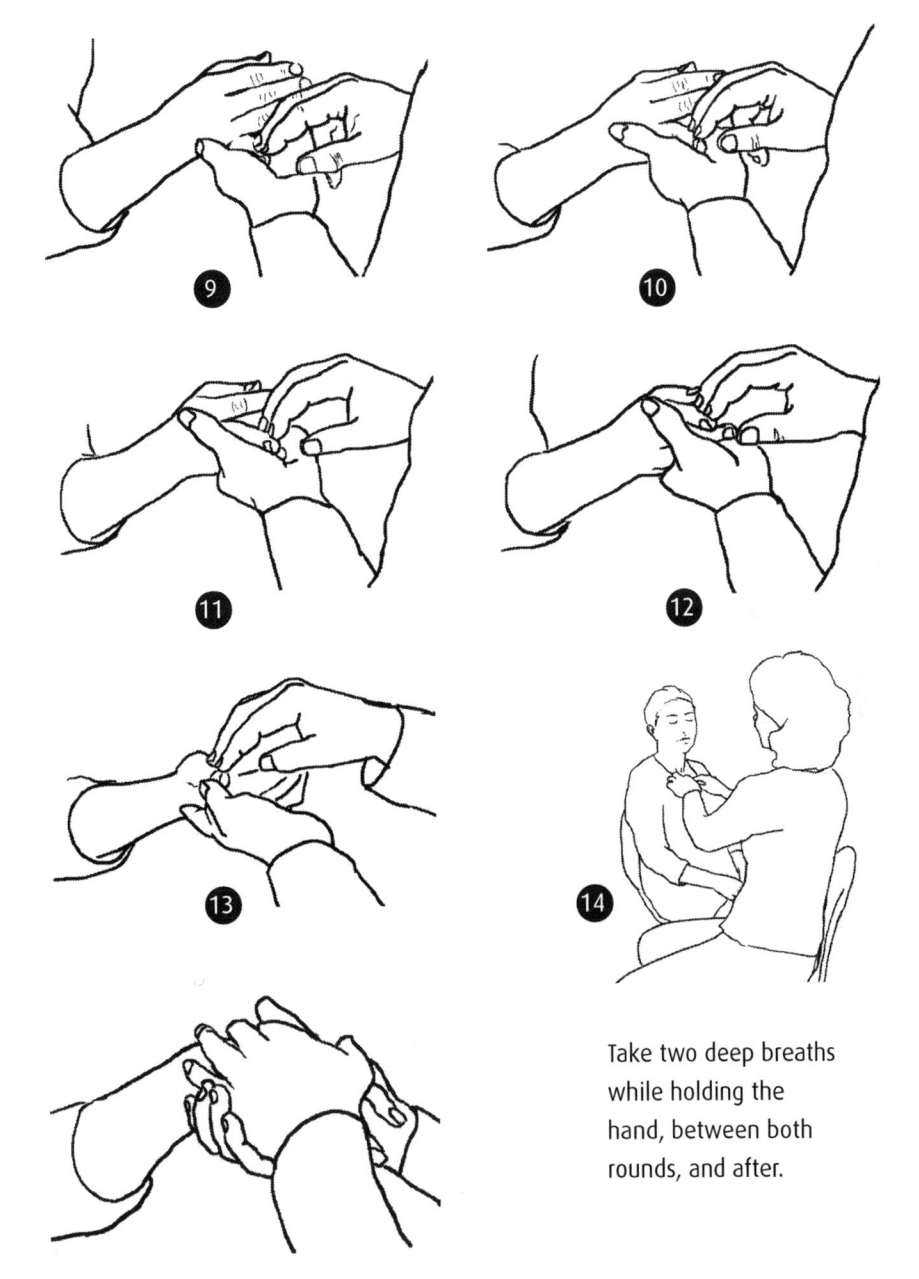

Take two deep breaths while holding the hand, between both rounds, and after.

Resolving Yesterday - First Aid for Stress and Trauma with TTT

A young learner in Sierra Leone.

Helping Children

The mechanics of trauma are different in children because their brains are not fully grown. Traumas experienced before language is learned are coded differently from those experienced after.

Tapping is a great tool with children. For them, the tapping procedure is like a game that they learn quickly. It is simple and it looks and feels like a funny exercise. They soon detect that it is calming, whether in Congo, Sweden or India. Children, just like adults, can do the tapping to themselves and their friends.

While doing the tapping the child's mind should be activated on whatever feeling or thought that is bothering them. With children you can simply ask them to tell you what has happened, regardless of whether it was during a day in school, during the escape from the village or when the earthquake started. When children tell their story, their mind will automatically become activated on what is making them upset, allowing the tapping procedure to work. When children don't feel like talking about something you can simply ask them "*If anything is bothering you, anything at all, what would that be?*" This is enough.

Trauma can be passed on from one generation to the next. For example, in Rwanda many children born after the genocide suffer from post-traumatic stress. They inherit the chemical landscape of their mother, and they hear the stories of traumatized parents in a society with fear of more violence.

Since traumatic stress can block our logical thinking, our hopes for the future and our ability to learn, it is of utmost importance to treat traumas in children, allowing them a healthy and worthy life.

Tapping Toto

When introducing a tapping we sometimes share this story:

Gunilla:

Some time ago when I was coming out from an internet café in Bukavu in eastern Congo, I saw somebody I recognized on the other side of the street. "Jambo Louis!" I shouted over the noise of the motorcycle taxis passing between us. Louis was a participant from one of our TTT trainings. He stopped, waved and made his way across the street through the traffic. This is what he told me:

"Last September my youngest son Toto was going to start school. I went with him on the first day. All the new pupils were supposed to answer some questions, like an exam, to check if they were ready for school.

There were a lot of people in front of the school and in the classrooms. I felt Toto slowing down and holding on to my hand tighter and tighter. It was like he was hiding behind me.

'Come Toto, let's go to your classroom', I said, but he continued dragging behind.

The classroom was jam packed with children and parents. At front was the teacher, a tall woman dressed in bright colors, overlooking the crowd.

I felt Toto pulling my hand: 'No, dad, please, I can't go in there…' Toto said with a terrified look in his eyes.

'What's happening, my son?' I asked him.

'I don't dare to go in there, please, dad, I want to go home', answered Toto almost crying.

At that moment I came to think about the "gorilla tapping" that we learned during the TTT training. I said to Toto: 'Come my boy, let's make ourselves brave like the big gorillas!'

I led Toto out of the classroom and started showing Toto the tapping on the chest. 'This is how the gorillas do, isn't it?' I said, 'Just do like me now.'

He nodded and started to imitate me. After tapping for a while I asked him: 'How do you feel?' He smiled and said 'I'm okay now.'

We went back to the classroom. When entering through the door, Toto let go of my hand and walked without hesitation through the crowd, up to the teacher. She asked him something in French, which is the language of the learned people in our country, but Toto answered in Swahili: 'Please Madame, could you say the questions to me in Swahili, French is difficult. '

The teacher looked surprised at Toto. Then she bent forward and lifted him up from the floor and said: 'You are a brave boy. Of course we can talk in Swahili.'

On A Chess Tournament for Kids

Another example of doing TTT with children comes from Sweden:

Ulf:

When my daughter was ten years old, her whole class participated in a yearly chess tournament for kids. They participate as a class, counting points from every individual game. This means that every child is partly responsible for the outcome of the class in each game. Imagine the pressure.

One boy got so nervous that he threw up. He cried and wanted to go home. This situation holds a lot of pressure on a kid this age – the class effort depended on him playing.

My wife, Melodie, tapped him as he was standing and crying, using a napkin to mop up the vomit. After two rounds she looked him in the eyes and asked *"Can you give it a try?"*

He turned around with a weak smile, nodded, played – and won. After this he has asked for a tapping every now and then before games, but most importantly, the whole class realized that it's ok to be nervous, and that there are things you can do about it. Simple things, like tapping.

Marie – A Session in Rwanda

Gunilla:
Nobody knew what happened to Marie during the genocide, except that she had been beaten repeatedly in the head with one of the heavy clubs the Interhamwe militia used for killing when there were no machetes available. She was beaten so badly that she was considered dead and left behind when others fled in panic from the church where hundreds of people had taken refuge. Churches had previously been safe places, but during the genocide people were slaughtered in churches as well. No place was safe at that time.

When Marie's brother opened the door 16 years later, he had a welcoming smile. We had come to see Marie. He removed the shirts he was busy ironing from the table in the small room and asked us to sit down.

According to tradition you always offer visitors something to drink. "*Do you want a glass of water?*" he asked. He told us Marie was in bed with one of her many severe headaches since the genocide.

"*Perhaps we should come another day when she feels better?*" I asked.

"*No, not at all, she really wants to try the treatment that I have told her about*", her brother said and showed us to her room.

Under an almost transparent sheet there was the shape of a small body, thin and curled up as a baby. Our colleague Robert Ntabwoba, who knew her from before, sat down beside her.

"*Marie, amakuru? How are you?*"

She did not answer but removed the sheet from her face and looked at us.

With a soft voice Robert explained what we could do for her and asked if she wanted us to start.

"*Yego*", she whispered. "*Ntakibazo.*" Yes, no problem.

Since Marie was so obviously connected to the emotions of her memories, having the headaches when the thoughts and feelings from the genocide came back, we did not need to ask her to think about her problems. She was already in touch with them.

I did a gentle tapping. Marie had her eyes closed and was laying still. After the third round Robert asked her how she felt. She didn't reply in words but opened her eyes and gave us a faint smile and murmured: "*Nimeza*" Fine. She turned towards the wall and seemed to fall asleep.

We didn't know for sure if Marie was properly helped by the tapping at this point, but she seemed calm. We didn't want to disturb her by asking questions and rating the pain. The answer would be obvious anyway, sooner or later.

We sat down and chatted a while with Marie's brother. He was very concerned about his sister, whom he had cared for just like the other four siblings since they were reunited after the genocide.

They had managed well in life and studies in spite of being orphans. It was only Marie who couldn't continue her education. She was too traumatized, as if she was not present in her own life.

After a couple of days I came back to check up on Marie. When I walked down the slope I saw her in the garden hanging clothes behind the house. When she saw me coming she put down the rest of the clothes in a bucket and gave me a warm hug.

She looked different: Her face was open, and what a smile! She had fixed her hair in plaits and wore a pretty and ironed blue jeans dress.

I asked if she still had "things to clear". She said "*Yes.*" and we did a new tapping. This time there was no need for explanations. She knew the procedure. She closed her eyes and let the tapping happen.

The brother came out of the house.

"*We never expected this, he said, Marie is doing so fine. She is taking responsibility for the household money and she has started training to become a hairdresser. It is amazing.*"

Little by little Marie changed. The headaches eventually disappeared, and the nightmares too. She even participated in the Memorial days held each year to commemorate the genocide, a huge suffering and re-traumatizing event for many, but no longer for her.

I meet Marie every time I come to Rwanda. She is a beautiful and well-functioning young woman, working in a hair salon. Imagine.

TTT over Skype

You can teach, train and perform TTT over Skype with a web cam. We recommend making sure there is somebody with the client that can be helpful if emotions get strong. As a part of the session we explain how they can continue to tap themselves as a tool for self-help afterwards.

Ulf:
This is a Skype session with a client that needed help with years of nightmares after his wife had committed suicide. It turned out that maybe this was not the reason for the nightmares, or maybe at least not the only one.

In these sessions I had a video connection so we could see each other. I asked the client to connect to the feelings of discomfort and when he said he could feel that feeling at the level of an 8 on a scale from 0–10 (the so called SUD scale that we mentioned before with 0 being no discomfort and 10 being the worst amount of discomfort) I asked him to do as I did and tapped myself through the procedure. As we went along I would remind him to stay in touch with the feeling and reassure him it was ok. If he went too far into the feeling I would pull him out ever so slightly by asking for a detail, a name or a place. Afterwards we evaluated how strong the feeling was, thinking about it in the exact same way he did before we started. Now the feeling was down to 2, maybe 1. I felt it was safe to trust that the client would continue and reach 0 on his own if he continued Trauma Tapping on the feeling himself. We did two sessions and the results evolved in three days, with a follow-up after half a year.

After some days he wrote me an email:

"Do you remember that, although I first called you for help with nightmares, a nightmare feeling lasting long into the day or all day, "day mares", uncontrolled tearfulness, which all seemed connected with my wife's suicide, visions of her last horrible months, her face at the morgue, my mistakes surrounding her *fatal depression etc. And then when you asked me at the beginning of our first session, what painful image first came to mind, it was my terror of being 'lost' during evacuation from London at age five during the Second World War.*

So which memories set off the nightmares? Maybe my wife's suicide, the worst thing that ever happened to me, and her, conjured up the nightmare I was living in, or maybe my childhood terror made it unbearable, or maybe the two traumas just ran into one? I don't know.

About 20 years ago, when I was suffering from a 'bleeding gut' I heard a BBC program about people suffering from similar pathologies, who, it turned out, had all, like me, suffered trauma 50 years earlier through the War! My colon is no longer bleeding, mainly through psychotherapies and meditation (although the gastroenterologists don't much like to 'let go'!) but it shows how long those wartime traumas can last.

At the time my wife was in the hospital, and, I thought, 'safe', and they phoned me to tell me she had 'attempted' suicide, and refused to tell me if she was dead. But after only one hour of the horrific three-hour journey to the hospital, I knew she was dead."

As you can tell there are many traumatic events layered here: The wife's suicide, the feeling that he may have been able to prevent it, the horrific three-hour journey to the hospital not knowing if she was dead or not–plus the childhood trauma of war 50 years earlier that may have set the conditions for this later trauma to evolve into post-traumatic stress in the form of nightmares and daycares.

These are his emails after two sessions. They show how memories stayed while emotional reactions gradually detached during the three days following the TTT intervention.

One day later

"I'd like to tell you about how it's going since your fantastic help. I don't want to burden you further, and there's no need to reply. I still have my eyes full of tears when I watch a film about love, separation, reuniting, someone lost found again, but I no longer feel stuck in a dead end – no escape. If it gets too hard, tapping on my eyebrows helps me to come back to earth."

Two days later
"I did as you said, and the first part of the night I slept without any dreams I could remember. Unfortunately I woke up about 2 hours before dawn, without having slept enough. So I tried to go back to sleep. But every time I started to doze off, I was reawakened by a '2 second nightmare' or a nightmarish vision (or occasionally a '2 second dream', not a nightmare). Stupidly, I didn't think of doing the tapping right away. I did it about 10 o'clock, after a rather nightmarish feeling since I got up at 6:35, and it has helped.
Thank you for your support. :)"

Four days later
"I had no nightmare last night! Just some light-hearted dreams!
    Thank you."

I asked if I can quote his emails for this book half a year later, and this was his answer:

Six months later
"I hope you are well. Of course you can quote me!
    I still have nightmares from time to time (I suppose everybody does) but they fade when I awake – nothing like what I went through before you helped me, when they were continual and continuous – lasting into, and often throughout, my waking days.
    And when I occasionally feel too much anxiety, or panic, I do the tapping and get serenity again. Thank you again, so much."

Teaching TTT on the Fly

We are always willing to teach the Trauma Tapping Technique, no matter where and with whom as long as the person being taught is willing to learn and share.

In our shortest moments we have been able to do a brief training in as little as half an hour, provided that the person learning has enough knowledge about emotional distress and experience and is keen enough to continue on their own.

This may sound careless, as if we are not taking our mission seriously and letting people with little knowledge deal with difficult problems, like trauma, and certainly it is much better if you can have a proper training with plenty of time, but life does not always offer that. You might save a life by teaching or doing TTT to somebody. Remember that we regard this as a first aid technique for everyone, not a replacement for other treatments if these are available.

Some of our trainings have been conducted under improvised forms, on a subway in New York or in the transit hall of an airport. We want to share some of these stories, hoping you will be inspired by the simplicity and potential of teaching TTT on the fly.

On A Subway to Harlem
Gunilla:
Hjalmar Joffre-Eichhorn works with the theatre for reconciliation in different parts of the world. For several years he has been based in Kabul in Afghanistan. During a meeting on reconciliation in New York Hjalmar asked if I wanted to join him for a theatre performance in the Latin American area of the city.

When we reached the subway, three of Hjalmar's Afghan theatre colleagues joined us. One of them, Salim Rajani, asked:

"Can you please teach me that Trauma Tapping? Hjalmar showed us once in Kabul but I don't really know how to do it properly."

Saleem Rajani from Afghanistan learning TTT on the subway train in New York.

"Of course", I said, *"But it has to be here because this is the only time we have together."* *"No problem!"* Salim replied.

It was rush hour on the New York subway train between Wall Street station and the Bronx. We found a seat at the window, and as I explained the theory involved I tapped the points on Salim. Just before reaching Bronx station Salim had finished tapping also on me. All in all we had used 25 minutes on the train ride to do the training.

A couple of weeks later I got an email from Salim, back in Kabul.
"Dear Gunilla

Thank you for teaching me the Tapping methodology and sending me your web-site address. I just had a training with victims of the war, mainly widows, in the west of Afghanistan and did Trauma Tapping. We used the TTT when they were telling their story. It was great and useful!

This is what some of the widows said:

'Now after the Tapping I really feel relaxed and as if something got released from my heart.'

'During the Tapping, I wanted to sleep and I felt very close to my partner who has been killed.'

Hope to see you again

Best regards Salim"

Some months later I wrote Salim to ask how things were going with the tapping:

'Today we use TTT after every single story, with the purpose of changing tears to energy. The situation in Afghanistan has brought so much tragedy that the war victims get shocked after sharing their personal story. TTT is the best technique for spiritual therapy and showing empathy to them. It switches the atmosphere to positive and creates a strong vision for raising their voices to get their rights met.'"

A Military Experience of TTT
Gunilla:
Paul had a long career in the military. He went to Lebanon as a UN soldier in 1983, and experienced situations that had haunted him since. He didn't recognize that he was traumatized until five years later when he started getting aggressive without any obvious reason. He couldn't concentrate on his work- intrusive images of what he had seen kept coming to his mind. Paul started self-medication with alcohol, and as a consequence lost his family, his work and eventually himself.

After some time he realized he had to do something to help himself. He travelled back to Lebanon to confirm that the danger was over. This calmed him down somewhat, but when we met he could still react to the memories of the images from the village where he had arrived just after a massacre, with blood and body parts all over the place. There was also a staged execution that kept showing up in dreams, and images of children the same age as his own scattered in that field, killed by land mines.

I met Paul at the coffee bar at the airport in Addis Ababa in Ethiopia.

"You know," he said, "there was no talk about those kind of traumatic reactions within the military by then. We were supposed to 'manage' the situations we were sent to deal with. That was our job. But many came back with emotional distress and trauma. And many suffered without looking for help or being offered any. Of the 15 in my platoon only four are still alive. Many committed suicide."

"I actually feel distressed right now. It comes and goes. I have been walking five turns round the airport to calm down", he said and ordered another beer.

I told him about our trauma work and the method we use. He got interested, for himself personally and for his colleagues in the land mine project he was working for who had also lived through different situations of war.

Paul looked doubtful when I told him how simple TTT is, but said he wanted to know more. We exchanged contacts. *"Let's see what we can do..."*

Then they called out my flight and asked the passengers to proceed to the gate. I paid for my coffee, took my bag and said goodbye to Paul.

On my way towards the gate a thought struck my mind:

'Why don't I ask if he wants to try a tapping session?'

I checked the time and hurried back to the coffee bar to see if he was still there. I found him at the same spot drinking his beer.

"Would you like me to show you the technique?"

"Yes, why not?' he answered, *"But where?'*

"It has to be here on one of the benches", I pointed out into the transfer hall, *"I don't have time to look for another place."*

"Okay, no problem."

On a bench in the middle of the stream of people moving from one gate to another I started explaining the Trauma Tapping to Paul. He brought up one of his distressing memories to his mind. After one round of Trauma Tapping he reacted like a balloon being punctuated, and with a deep sigh his shoulders came down. After the second round came tears. I continued until he got completely calm. When he opened his eyes, he somewhat looked with amazement at me and gave me a hug while uttering: "Thank you!"

He told me about the images that had come to his mind during the Trauma Tapping, the horrific images of the massacre and the mock execution, and how they lost their power over him, and became diffuse and distant.

In the next moment realizing that I had to dash off to the gate.

"I will send you an email!" Paul shouted after me.

One week later this email came:

"Hi Gunilla,

This is unbelievable! After the tapping you did for me at the airport I slept like a baby on the plane. I think it has never happened before. And since then I have slept every night without using alcohol at all. I can't remember how long time ago that was possible. If somebody would have told me these kind of reactions after a treatment like that I would not have believed it was true. But you have made me a believer. I am utterly grateful for what you did for me. I will talk to my colleagues and superiors and see if we can implement this in our work. Thank you again."

I wrote back to congratulate his resilience and strength for healing. When talking over the phone some time later Paul told me some more:

"I have much more energy now. I write my reports so fast that my superiors get surprised. No nightmares any more. This also means that my wife can sleep now. Before she would wake up when I kept moving restlessly during the night and mourn in my sleep.

I am much more balanced in my mood. I don't get angry easily like before neither at work nor at home. I can tell you my wife is very happy! I feel like a disarmed land mine. I am not dangerous any more. Not to myself or to others.

I keep telling people in my organization about my experience and many are interested also after reading your website.

Nobody could be a better advertiser about this than me. If I would not have experienced it, I would not believe it was possible to heal in this way."

Combining TTT with Other Treatments

Be creative and see how you can blend TTT into whatever type of treatment or therapy you regularly use. It should be quite easy to accomplish.

Using TTT with talking therapies

Most types of traditional talk based, or cognitive therapies, can benefit from adding a sensory technique like TTT when an emotional distress is triggered - since it allows the distress response to be deconditioned. Once the emotional response is handled, the cognitive system will be ready to continue processing the issue.

Using TTT with hypnotherapy

Hypnotherapy is a great tool for opening the doors to the subconscious and allowing a client to find the strategies, connections and solutions they have not been able to locate in their reflective conscious state of mind. There are many different ways of using the hypnotic state of suggestibility, but they all have one thing in common: they are reaching the mind through the language center of the brain. Combining this process with TTT makes it possible to reach the mind also through the sensory system. These are some ideas on the use of TTT in combination with hypnotherapy:

As an induction

It is a great time saver with analytical clients who want to stay in control by saying:

"*Let's wait with the hypnotic induction, allow me instead to show you a relaxation method that you can use as a First Aid for yourself when you need to level out stress and unpleasing emotions*".

Usually they are in trance after ten minutes or less.

During a session
Sometimes a client can trigger a strong stress response while exploring earlier or suppressed events in trance. To softly say *"I will now tap your forehead as we continue"* and start the TTT procedure from there, while explaining what will happen next to keep their sense of safety, allows the session to continue without having to go through the abreaction, and still resolving the underlying mechanism.

During the introductory interview
If an emotional response is activated during a pre-treatment interview it is a great opportunity to apply TTT. Many core issues can be cleared up, and the client will be moving into a relaxed and lighter trance, allowing for a natural progression into the hypnotherapy session.

Using TTT with massage therapy
It is not uncommon for emotional distress to be triggered during massage therapy. For a trained therapist it is easy to incorporate TTT for the emotional issue as part of the massage therapy, and then move back to treating the body symptoms.

Using TTT during pregnancy and labour
TTT is a wonderful tool for calming down the nervous system and helping mothers, fathers and babies during the pregnancy and also during childbirth. It is easy for the midwife or a relative to provide the technique.

Using TTT in dentistry
When there is anxiety in a dental care situation, applying TTT in the dentist chair prior to the oral examination will put the person at ease, lessen the anxiety and the perception of pain or discomfort.

Metaphors of Healing

In Africa and elsewhere people often explain their experiences of Trauma Tapping with poetic words. One of our favorite metaphors was told by a widow called Marie-Christine during a training in Kibungo, Rwanda:

"I feel as if I have been walking up a mountain for many, many years. Now I can finally sit down and rest and even enjoy the view overlooking the landscape below."

Metaphors are very interesting from a healing point of view. If you can help a person find a metaphor for what is troubling them, he or she can sometimes find a solution for the troubles by changing the metaphor.

For example, if a person says that he or she feels like there is a weight on the chest, pressing the air out, you could ask what kind of weight it is. This will make him or her explore it, and provide more details, like *"it is like the foot of an elephant, but it is not moving"*. By asking them to *"Imagine something that can move that elephant!"* can prompt their creative mind to come up with the solution of luring away the elephant with a bag of peanuts, and then imagining what that will feel like. This will allow their creative mind to imagine what healing can feel like in a playful way that isn't stopped by critical and pragmatic thoughts like *"You cannot just lure away your anxiety as if it was an elephant, using a bag of peanuts – or can you?"*

You may be amazed at the power of metaphors once you start exploring this.

There is an African metaphor for trauma:

"A man who has once been tossed by a buffalo, when he sees a black ox, thinks it's another buffalo".

Other metaphors that we have gathered from people experiencing TTT:
"It feels like a wind came through my mind "
"A burden fell off my shoulders."
"This is like anesthesia, I feel as if those problems of mine walked out of my mind."
"I feel awake for the first time since very long."
"If I do this every day I might go to heaven without dying."
"I had something hard in my heart. But now it has melted."
"It feels like water flowing in my body now, it dissolves something that was stuck there."

The Metaphor of Jacques

Jacques was one of the first orphans to experience Trauma Tapping in Rwanda. Today he has a Master in Public Health. This is Jacques' story:

"Before I learned the tapping I could not think about those loved ones that I lost during the genocide. It felt like entering a dark fearful forest, not knowing what kind of danger awaited me there. I avoided the forest because it was too painful. But avoiding it also meant that I could not think about my parents and family. This made me feel very bad. Because you know for us Africans it is very important to connect with our ancestors. Therefore I felt like I betrayed them.

But after getting to know this Tapping technique things have changed. The forest has turned into a garden with flowers and different kind of trees. In this garden I can sit down with my family and feel we are all together again. It is a true relief."

The philosophical farmer

Another of our favorite metaphors of healing is the story of the Taoist farmer from fourth century B.C. by Lao Tzu:

The farmer had only one horse, and one day the horse ran away. The neighbors came to condole over his terrible loss. The farmer said, *"What makes you think it is so terrible?"*

A month later, the horse came home – this time bringing with her two beautiful wild horses. The neighbors became excited at the farmer's good fortune. "Such lovely strong horses!" The farmer said, *"What makes you think this is good fortune?"*

The farmer's son was thrown from one of the wild horses and broke his leg. All the neighbors were very distressed. Such bad luck! The farmer said, *"What makes you think it is bad?"*

A war came, and every able-bodied man was conscripted and sent into battle. Only the farmer's son, because he had a broken leg, remained. The neighbors congratulated the farmer. *"What makes you think this is good?"* said the farmer with a smile.

Going with the Flow

Another Taoist story tells of an old man who accidentally fell into the river rapids leading to a high and dangerous waterfall. Onlookers feared for his life. Miraculously, he came out alive and unharmed downstream at the bottom of the falls. People asked him how he managed to survive.

"I accommodated myself to the water, not the water to me. Without thinking, I allowed myself to be shaped by it. Plunging into the swirl, I came out with the swirl. This is how I survived."

The Dizziness Disappeared

Gunilla:
I treated David, a former soldier in South Sudan. We met during a training of 200 Peace Mobilizers in the capital Juba. During the training we did a workshop on TTT since trauma is a huge problem in South Sudan after 50 years of war, atrocities and subordination from other people.

After the workshop David came to me for an individual session. We had already met some days before when I accompanied him to the health clinic because he was suffering from a severe headache and feeling so very dizzy that he was afraid of falling. While waiting outside the clinic David started telling me of his experiences during the war: violent situations nobody should have to live through. The doctor finally attended to David, gave him a prescription of Paracetamol and told him to drink more water. We went out into the almost burning sun and crossed the street to get the medicine at the pharmacy.

When David came to me after the TTT workshop he said: *"When you were talking about the symptoms of trauma I recognized myself. I have several more of them. And honestly, I still have that headache and that dizziness like the other day. I think they are also symptoms of my experiences. Can you help me?"*

I asked David to sit down on a chair in an office room where we could be alone. I asked him to focus lightly on the worst event of the war that kept coming to his mind. He closed his eyes. After one round of tapping his chest deflated like a balloon in a deep sigh. In the middle of the second round he suddenly opened his eyes widely and said: *"It's gone!! The heavy feeling in my head is gone."* He shook my hand and left hastily.

The following day I saw him passing towards the lecture hall. He waved and shouted: *"No more dizziness. No headache! Thank you!"*

A workshop at St Vincent SMI School at Pala, India.

TTT WITH GROUPS

The Starfish Thrower

One summer's morning a little girl was walking on a long, winding beach. She came across a starfish that had been washed ashore and was now wriggling and drying up in the hot sun. She reached down, gently picked up the starfish by one of its five points, and tossed it back into the sea. The little girl smiled and continued walking along the beach. But after a few steps, she found another starfish. It too was dying in the sun. No sooner had she tossed this one back, when she came across another starfish, and then another one. Each time she found one she picked it up and tossed it back into the sea.

She reached the top of a sand dune and came to a sudden stop. What she saw below startled and amazed her. Stretching out in front of her were hundreds upon hundreds, maybe even thousands, of dying starfish washed up on the beach. Suddenly, she exploded into action and began to toss as many starfish as possible, one by one, back to the sea.

She was so busy tossing back the starfish, that she hadn't even noticed that a person had stopped to watch her. Soon a small crowd had gathered. Some started pointing at the little girl and laughed.

"*That little girl's crazy*", said one.

"*I know*", said another.

"*Doesn't she know that every summer thousands of starfish get washed up on the beach and die? It's just the way things are.*"

"*There are so many starfish. She can't possibly make any difference.*"

The little girl was still too busy tossing back starfish to notice them. Finally, one man decided he had seen enough. He walked over to the little girl.

"*Little girl,*" he said, "*there are thousands of starfish washed up on the beach. You can't possibly hope to make any real difference. Why don't you give up, and go play on the beach with the other children?*"

The little girl's smile suddenly vanished. She noticed the crowd of people for the first time, and she realized they had been laughing at her. And now they had fallen silent, awaiting her answer to the man's question.

She was hot. She was tired and close to tears. She began to think that maybe he was right. Maybe they were all right. She had been tossing back starfish for what seemed like hours, and yet a carpet of starfish still covered the beach. How could she have possibly thought she could make a difference? Her arms fell limp at her sides, and the starfish she was holding fell back to the hot sand. She started to walk away.

Then suddenly she stopped, turned around, reached back down, and picked up the starfish she had dropped. She swung back her arm and tossed the starfish as far as she possibly could. When it landed with a plop, she turned to the man, and with a huge smile on her face she said:

"I made a difference to that one!"

Inspired, a little boy emerged from the crowd, and he too picked up a starfish and sent it soaring back to the sea.

"And I made a difference to that one!" he said.

One by one every person in the crowd, old and young, joined in sending dying starfish back to the sea, calling: *"I made a difference to that one!"* with each toss.

After a while the voices began to quiet down. The little girl became aware of this, and she wondered if the people were getting tired or discouraged. And so she looked across the beach. What she saw startled and amazed her. All the starfish were gone!

Many years later, another little girl was walking down the same beach. She reached the top of a sand dune, and came to a sudden stop. As far as her eyes could see, there were people tossing starfish into the sea. Curious, she approached an older man. *"Could you please tell me sir, why is everyone tossing starfish back into the sea?"*

The man, many years earlier, had been the little boy who was the first one to step forward and help the little girl save the starfish. *"Little girl"*, he replied, *"each year, when a summer storm washes thousands of starfish onto the beach, the entire town comes out to toss them all back to the sea. You see, we learned one summer, many years ago, that when we all work together, we can actually make a huge difference."*

Adapted from Loren Eiseley

A parents group in Ngororero, Rwanda.

Teaching and Treating in Groups

"I attended the sessions given by your team. It was a great experience. I hope to use it in my therapy. I could see in your team a prefect blending of stage art, music and simple & logical use of Trauma Tapping Techniques. I appreciate very much your desire to help people in distress. Hope to keep in touch with you."

Reverend Dr. Jose Puthenveed

TTT is very well suited for group settings, which is one of the advantages with the method. We teach TTT in groups more often than we treat people individually. We want to use the multiplier effect as much as possible, allowing the ones who learn TTT to pass on the knowledge to others. We want to empower people and make them realize that their fingertips are tools for healing.

We usually say:

"This method is a gift to you. It is a gift too valuable to be kept in your drawer, under your mattress or on the shelf. Pass it on. Share it with others."

Advantages of Group Trainings

We find group trainings to be a great way to teach TTT.
- The setup of learning TTT in a group takes focus away from individual problems, we are all sharing a learning experience, some of us are also resolving emotional issues.
- The dynamics of learning together with other people, seeing their reactions and sharing their thoughts is often a stronger learning experience than learning alone.
- Group trainings are time- and cost efficient, since many can learn and be treated at the same time.

Know Your Audience

The way we do a group-training depends on the experience and knowledge of the participants. A group of former child soldiers, women subjected to gender based violence, orphans or refugees have the direct experience of trauma while counselors and other professionals will usually have a secondary experience and more theoretical knowledge. In some countries we focus more on creating relief from emotional distress in general, than on trauma from war.

How Much Time Is Available?

Our way of conducting a workshop depends on the time available. Teaching only the Trauma Tapping procedure itself doesn't take long; it can be done in 15–30 minutes. We have done it in ten minutes when necessary.

On other occasions we have done trainings over several days, which gives much more opportunities to discuss and for the participants to learn from each other. We then include more theoretical knowledge about the principles of dealing with post-traumatic stress. We also teach additional exercises and treatments such as Blow Out, Gorilla Tapping and Do-in.

Example of a Group Training

This is a suggestion for how you can conduct a group training:

1. Introduce the technique as a psychological First Aid, and a method to relax the body and the mind. Tell the group about some of the experiences people have described in this book, and your own experiences of using TTT.
2. Show the tapping points on yourself and/or on a drawing, a blackboard or flip chart. The basic material can be downloaded from our website.
3. Start with a self-tapping by doing the tapping procedure together with the participants. Once this is done, ask one of the participants to lead the tapping, this usually makes the participants more alert.
4. Ask for reactions and comments.
5. Show how to treat another person by asking for a volunteer, often many like to be treated, and remember to use two chairs in parallel to each other as described earlier.
6. Let the participants practice treating each other two by two if they seem to have grasped the method. If they seem unsure ask them to treat each other

three by three so they can change between the roles of tapper, being tapped and supervisor.
7. Ask for reactions and comments.

During all the practice go around and assist where assistance is needed.

Variations
From this basic training there are innumerable variations.
　　Depending on the time available we also cover as much as possible of the following theoretical topics:
- How we become traumatized
- What are symptoms of traumatic stress
- Traditional and conventional ways of treating trauma
- Attitude, confidence and congruency
- Basic ethics
- Things to consider when treating soldiers and survivors of sexual abuse
- Other relaxation and body awareness exercises

It is an important part of the learning procedure to let the participants share their knowledge and experiences.

TTT street music workshop at our trauma center in Bukavu, Congo.

Musicians from TTT street music workshop in Bukavu, Congo.

The Somatic Poem

This poem is specifically designed for working with groups, with gestures and words carefully chosen to activate a state of mind where change is possible and TTT can be taught and applied to a group.

It is performed all together in call and response. Everybody follows the leader.

Imagine. Imagine a rain (arms up to the sky)
Imagine a healing rain that falls on your head (touch head)
That washes your head, also on the inside (touch head)
Washes away your images (touch eyes)
Your sounds (touch ears)
The pain in your heart (touch chest)
The burdens on your shoulders (touch shoulders and sides)
And washes it all to the ground (bend down)
And then... you take a step forward (dramatic step forward)
And another (dramatic step forward)
Leaving the burdens behind

The combination of physical movement and spoken or sung words is a double activation. Seeing it being done is a third activation. By taking a step forward you decontaminate your past and physically leave it behind before you start the tapping.

Women singing to gather people for a workshop in Sierra Leone.

Trauma Tapping in Song and Dance

In Sierra Leone we experienced for the first time how Trauma Tapping easily can be adapted into the traditional ways of healing, the dancing and singing. Combining TTT with music and dance makes the tapping an even more efficient tool. Music and dance open up the connection between the two hemispheres of the brain and the "door" to the unconscious mind where the memories are stored. Dancing often brings trance, and trance is the gateway to the unconscious mind.

To heal the traumas of the war, dancing and signing may not be sufficient in itself. But together with the tapping or other similar interactions the impact is more profound. Music and singing also makes it easier for many to remember the sequence of Trauma Tapping. This is what happened in Sierra Leone:

A TTT Song in Sierra Leone
Gunilla:
It is already midday and hot when we arrive in the village Woama in the south of Sierra Leone. We are met by the woman chief dressed in a beautiful flower patterned dress and the same cloth wrapped around her head. She is big and proud:

"*How di bodi?*" she greets us in Kriol with a firm handshake asking for our names while having steady eye contact.

In the next moment a whole group of women appears singing with high pitch voices accompanying themselves with calabash maracas and rattles made from animal jaw bones. They show us around the village, singing and dancing, to gather the women for the meeting under a big kola nut tree. More women join, many have come walking three-four hours from neighboring villages. Finally over 150 are there. They all belong to the "Peace Mothers" initiated by Fambul Tok, an organization dedicated to bring people together for reconciliation using traditional ways, like gathering under the village tree and the bonfire to talk and exchange ideas and settle conflicts.

We were invited to Sierra Leone to do Trauma Tapping since trauma is a big problem after the so called Blood Diamond War that devastated the country and traumatized the population between 1991 and 2001. The name reflects that incomes from diamond and gold mines kept the conflict going. This is a parallel to what happens in eastern Congo today. According to statistics 80 percent of the population fled their home and became refugees. Many children were used as soldiers in the rebel groups.

The inner wounds are still there, but people seem to long for reconciliation and ways to heal the memories of the past atrocities. There is an obvious willingness to change.

The staff of Fambul Tok introduced us to the women:

"Our friends have come to give you something for the peace in your hearts."

When we had gone through the procedures of the Trauma Tapping somebody started a tune and in few minutes a song was composed to make it easy to remember the sequence of tapping points for the treatment. A drum, a jerrycan and a calabash maracas joined in and we all moved along in the Trauma Tapping, singing something like: "under the eye, under the nose… we do the tapping… and then we breathe, breathe…" in the local language.

In trance we moved together all of us, singing, dancing, tapping and laughing!

Afterwards we were all sweating. One of the women chiefs exclaimed: *"I feel happy, happy, happy!"* Stretching her arms up in the air. The first Trauma Tapping Song was created.

TTT in a song at the rehabilitation center for child soldiers

Gunilla:

I was walking along the main road in Bukavu with our colleague Germando Barathi. The sun was blazing and the cars and taxis were crisscrossing between the potholes in the red dirt road.

"Wouldn't it be good with a song about the TTT?" Germando asked.

"What a brilliant idea!" I replied with my experiences from how TTT was turned into a song in Sierra Leone fresh in mind.

"Everybody loves singing here in Congo. That will make it easier to remember the Trauma Tapping."

"I will write one today", he promised.

We decided to meet the following day at the rehabilitation center for child soldiers to practice.

Germando was already rehearsing his TTT-song when I opened the red iron gate and entered the rehabilitation center compound. Some of the former child soldiers had joined him in the singing. The song was simple and easy to remember. We formed a circle and started following Germando while tapping and singing over and over again. One of the boys ran to get a drum. Finally the young boys knew the lyrics and the gestures well enough for us to film. You can check the result on our website.

We have used this song many times since, especially for trainings but also projecting the video at conferences to show ways to spread TTT. We have also found new ways to develop the combination of Trauma Tapping and music.

We have encouraged those who are musicians to compose Trauma Tapping songs, and more songs have been created since. In Africa, like in other places, people love singing. I have never heard anybody say "I don't know how to sing" there, which often happens in Sweden. Therefore Trauma Tapping songs are attractive and give good results.

Another colleague, Ajing Chol Giir, did a song during a training we had in South Sudan. He is using it to spread TTT in Dinka-speaking communities. After Ajing started using the song he wrote:

"All the children are singing the song and so do the alcoholics in the local bars. They too are traumatized."

In Rwanda, Dieudonné Munyanshoze and John Bizimana have composed a song called *Fingertips Heal Trauma* together with us to spread the message that healing is possible. Dieudonné is one of the most popular singers in Rwanda and is often engaged in different ceremonies in commemoration of the genocide of 1994 in Rwanda. Even though it is 20 years ago as we write this, people still suffer from symptoms of trauma. The songs can be found at our website.

City of Joy - Highlight of My Life
Ulf:

Without doubt one of the most memorable moments of my life as both a musician and a Trauma Tapper comes from our visit to The City Of Joy in Bukavu. This is the project of the legendary activist, play writer and defender of women's rights: Eve Ensler, where 90 young women who have been sexually abused, many with children of rape, are given a safe haven for six months. During this time they can heal physically and mentally, learn a profession, receive health care and learn about their rights.

At the gates there is a large vagina painted around the door. The original idea of Eve Ensler when she wrote the now famous *Vagina Monologues* was to focus on the most violated part of the female anatomy. She was convinced nobody would take them seriously, but they are now among the most played scripts in the world and have generated millions of dollars to her projects like City Of Joy.

For once we cannot document our workshop, because cameras are not allowed in the City Of Joy fully understandable considering the situation and background of the people there.

We are greeted by 45 of the young women in a large half circle of chairs, doing their special greeting, clapping hands six times in the rhythm of 3 + 3, and then holding them out "for you" and then six times and holding the hands to themselves "for me". This greeting is so powerful that we have adopted it for all our workshops since.

What followed was the most intense and open minded workshop of Trauma Tapping I have been through. We ended up testing our somatic poem as a setup for group teaching. We added in our extra repertoire of release techniques such as Blow Out for pent up anger and Do-in self massage for balancing the body-mind. In the end I brought out my piano and we did a call and response session where they were so synchronized that we ended up call and response dancing in a frenzy to a point of powerful and energetic calm. All in all this was a great way to conduct a group training, especially since the musical interaction is known to activate more of the human brain than any other activity, creating a high energy state of mind.

> "Women at City of Joy practice trauma tapping technique for their healing. The impact of Trauma Tapping is efficient, edifying, and reality proven. Results are seen in the testimonies of women who heal in the face of the impossible. TTT, among other approaches we use at City of Joy, is a response to the worries that women who have known a hell of a life have.
>
> There are testimonies from the women of City of Joy that when this technique is applied "hope and energy are recovered, and many changes become visible". Some women who are exhausted before the practice are more audacious to take initiative in the group and are excited to administer the same technique to other needy, traumatized persons."
>
> Christine Shuler Deschryver, Director at the City of Joy
> *Resolving Yesterday - First Aid for Stress and Trauma with TTT*

Making a TTT Song

This is a background and description for creating a song that can be used to teach and train TTT.

TTT can be applied in three basic ways, as a:
- Self-treatment
- First aid treatment of somebody else
- Group teaching and treatment

The group treatment with TTT is pretty unique. There are few, if any, other ways to treat trauma with large numbers of people simultaneously. Doing it combined with music also makes it simple to follow, simple to remember and pleasant. When considering the design of a TTT song, keep in mind that TTT is based on doing things in a sequence: connect, tap, breathe, tap and breathe a second time.

This is the sequence we propose for a TTT song session

1. **Connect**
   Activate a state of mind that relates to the symptoms and/or to what may have caused them. It is not necessary to go deep into the emotion – just connecting lightly.
2. **Tap**
   Apply the TTT by tapping two fingers (self or by somebody else) on the 14 tapping points, around 15 times per point.
3. **Breathe**
   Take two deep breaths, where the exhale is longer than the inhale.
4. **Repeat tap and breathe**
   Repeat steps 2 and 3 once. It is crucial that the technique is applied at least twice.

When incorporating TTT into a song you may want to decide if the song is supposed to work with visual input from the singer showing the tapping points, or if the text of the song needs to describe the points verbally as they go along.

Also consider integrating as many call and response actions as possible, they create a synchronicity within the group rehearsing it.

Poem and Song in a Session

Somatic poem (setup) + tapping + breathing + tapping + breathing

In some way it is necessary to connect as individuals to each emotion that is intended to be treated. One way that we have found working really well is the Somatic Poem we designed for this. (See Somatic Poem of Connection.)

We recommend a so called call and response setup, where the singer/leader taps first, and then asks the crowd to follow.

Tap on your karate point, or the side of your hand, using two fingers
Now tap on your eyebrows where they meet your nose, using two fingers
Now tap on the bone, at the sides of your eyes
Now tap on the bone, under your eyes
Now tap under your nose
On your chin
Under your collarbone
Under your arm
On your little finger, on top of the side of the nail
On your ring finger, on top of the side of the nail
On your middle finger, on top of the side of the nail
And your index finger, on top of the side of the nail
And your thumb, on top of the side of the nail
And now under your collarbone again

Now take a deep breath, hold your breath a second, and breathe out sloooooooowly.

Now let's repeat the full procedure once more (repeat all points).
At the end, the somatic poem can be repeated to allow everyone to reconnect to the cleaning rain and take two steps away into the future.

Ideas that may be useful

Show by doing. Hands can be held like in prayer, starting at your chest, breathing in while stretching out the arms in the air, and then lowering the hands and arms down the sides, as if swimming.

The inhale and exhale can be supported by a tone or instrument doing an upwards then downwards scale.

Words that are nice to include in the song:
- TTT
- Healing is possible
- Trauma healing is possible, maybe easier than you think?
- You can help yourself
- You can help your people

By mentioning symptoms those who do not understand how trauma can manifest itself may become interested. This may also be part of the somatic poem, or a rap section:
- When you have headache or can't sleep
- When you are feeling alone and afraid
- When your heart beats hard and your stomach hurts

If the song is used in an area with conflicting parties, it may be useful to include aspects of the conflicting parties. Is it possible to include a guest artist from both sides of any ongoing conflict?

TTT workshops are often concluded with dancing, here at Musanze, Rwanda.

Fatumeh, a Survivor of Sexual Violence

Fatumeh took part in a group training where the TTT song was rehearsed over ten times. The remarkable part of her story, besides the actual healing, is that she was treated by the process of rehearsing the song and gestures that incorporate the Trauma Tapping.

"It all happened ten years ago. We were together at home my parents and my three younger sisters. I was 14 at that time. After eating we went to sleep as usual, but that night the village was attacked by soldiers. They came also to our house and killed my mother and father and my three sisters in front of my eyes. They didn't kill me but took me to the forest and kept me there for four nights. They raped me, and when they had finished they just left me there unconscious.

I was saved by a shepherd who came grazing his cows where I was laying. He brought me to a health center in the next community. They tried to treat me but I was out of my mind. I was living in my memories like a crazy person. They sent me to the mental health clinic in Goma. I got some medicine to calm me down and for a while I felt a bit better. But after some time I got crazy again. They also found that I was pregnant. When I had given birth to the child I was in really bad shape. I could not breastfeed. Actually, I didn't want to see the child, I hated that baby who was born from that violence.

During several years I was in and out of clinics. On and off medicines, but the nightmares continued. I got crazy so many times. I didn't heal.

One day when my child came from school he said that the kids had bullied him for having a father who is an enemy and a mother who had been raped. I got so furious and threw a big stone at his head. You know, I could have killed him when I heard him say that. I thought it was the fault of the child that I felt the way I felt. I thought to myself:

'That child comes from the family who killed my parents and sisters. I don't want him!'

He reminded me of all the bad things that had happened. I was full of hate for him, myself, and for the whole world.

You know, by now I have been sick for so long. I have been living in my nightmares of what happened no matter what kind of treatment I got.

Even now last Saturday, here at City of Joy, I was running around in the compound, tearing off my clothes, screaming and beating the others. I didn't know what I was doing.

But yesterday when we were having this training of TTT and you said:

'With this technique you can help yourself', it made me think: 'I have got so many treatments and nothing has helped me. If with this technique I can help myself then let me try! Let me do this seriously!'

And I did. After doing the tapping and learning the tapping song it was as if a wind came through me and removed all the bad things within me. What was frozen in me started to melt.

The night after the training I slept well, so well that somebody had to wake me up in the morning. I felt like waking up to a new world. Now I feel well for the first time in a very long time. The heavy burden that I have been carrying in my head is gone. I can see things with other eyes now.

I even feel I can love my child. I will fight for the rights of these children, like my son, who has no father, to be accepted as any other child in our society. I want to work for creating peace in our country. I thank you for bringing this treatment to us! We will give it to others."

A secondary class learning TTT in Mbogo, Rwanda.

The Invisible Beauty of TTT

The highest form of ignorance is when you reject something you don't know anything about.

Our experience is that many humanitarian organizations and health institutions think that post-traumatic stress is difficult to heal, and needs be treated over long time or medicated individually.

We see a different reality where the power to heal trauma in a simple and efficient way even with large numbers of people on a national level is fully possible, and can be handled by the members of that community or nation.

So far, we have not found a method that can replace what we have been able to do with TTT – both individually and with large groups, over language barriers and in music. There are other methods that can heal traumatic stress, and some are more closely related to TTT than others (See: An Overview of PTSD Treatments). They all have a lot in common, although there are some important differences, mainly how the technique is set up, taught and spread. Most of these differences are explained in the chapter "The Evolution of TTT".

The main reasons why we prefer to teach and train TTT are these:

- **Empowerment:** We want to give a tool to the people who need it, and making them realize that they can help themselves, their family, friends and their community. They can pass TTT on. They can become the person that helps, instead of continuing being the victim waiting for a help that may never arrive.
- **Simplicity:** TTT is simple enough to remember, even for a traumatized person. Even for a person that maybe never went to school. This is why we keep it simple. Perhaps we could make it even more efficient for certain people, but at the cost of reaching less of those in need of it. Simple is good. The results we are getting are more than just good enough.

- **Communication:** In countries like Congo, where there are over 450 languages. Any spoken element of therapy has to pass through this bottleneck. Refugees coming to other countries carrying traumatic experiences have difficulties finding psychological support in their own language. This does not apply to TTT. The amount of translation needed to communicate the technique and conduct a group workshop is minimal. It is so minimal that a mime artist can do it. Imagine.
- **Multiplication:** You can easily reach a lot of people. We have simulated a situation where we teach 40 people in a refugee camp, and ask them to teach or treat 5 people each, reaching hundreds in a very short time.
- **Group treatment and training:** Imagine being able to provide a treatment and training for a group from 10 to 200, or as many as there are in a stadium, maybe thousands, at the same time. The reason why this is possible with TTT is because it is content-free: The method does not require speaking about each person's specific experience and trauma – it is focused on accessing the feelings involved and resolving them.
- **Minimal requirements:** The only costs involved in spreading TTT are transportation, food and water. It is a technique that can be taught in any environment. TTT has been taught at bus stops and subways, under trees, in schools, in conference halls, on boats and in restaurants.
- **Transferability:** TTT is simple, has a low requirement of schooling, background and language and there are no costs or other requirements, allowing us to spread TTT using printed calendars, videos (for example on Youtube), posters, leaflets, songs, dance and even using a megaphone.

The Magic of Empowerment

"The best way to find yourself is to lose yourself in the service of others."
Mahatma Gandhi

We have been teaching the Trauma Tapping Technique to many people who previously were considered as victims: for example women subjected to sexual violence in eastern Congo where rape is used as a weapon in warfare.

Being treated as a victim and internalizing this concept can be devastating for the self-esteem of a person. When looking for help at a local or international organization or hospital it is often required to repeat the story of what happened, over and over again, each time deepening the neurological pathways of this identity. Finally the victim's identity becomes just that: being a victim.

When learning a technique like TTT these things can change dramatically. Suddenly these victims can help not only themselves, but also others who need to relax their nervous systems from the pains of certain memories. The possibility of assisting victims to become healers is one of the main reasons for us to do this work. The empowerment of helping others often reinforces your own healing process. To help others is to help yourself!

During a TTT workshop in Bukavu in eastern Congo, Chantal, one of the women in a micro credit project, told us her story: She had fled her village after her husband was killed. Bukavu had become in a way like an urban refugee camp: Everyday people came hoping to find a safer place. Different armed groups were making life unbearable for the ordinary people in the villages. With guns as their means of power the rebels and soldiers loot and kill and most of all they rape women and girls to disintegrate the society.

Following the TTT workshop, Chantal said:

"We who don't have anything, who live like rats in houses with leaking roofs and hardly enough food to feed our kids – we have become healers! Not even in the hospital did we get this kind of medicine. We are proud to be able to help ourselves, and others, with the problems so many of us live with inside."

TTT in Church, School, Prison and Workplaces

Try to put a peaceful heart on the daily schedule. We propose every organization where people have a natural meeting point in the schedule: Add TTT as a group exercise! It will only take ten minutes and the results will affect everybody involved. It can be done as part of mass in church, as a morning exercise in school or anytime there is a normal meeting.

In Kenya our colleague John Njoroge started doing TTT before the practice of his choir and noticed that the quality of the singing improved.

Nabino Bahamanywa is the principal of a University in Bukavu. After a personal experience of how TTT released the traumatic stress he carried from living in the conflict zone of Congo, he went back and added it to the schedule for both students and teachers as a daily exercise in the morning. After three weeks they noticed the noise and aggression levels had lowered significantly, whereas learning levels had improved.

TTT in Rwandan Prisons

Thousands of perpetrators from the Genocide in 1994 are in prison. Theses prisoners suffer from trauma as well as their victims, creating problems for their rehabilitation and their possibilities to reconcile with and in society. Many of the survivors as well as the perpetrators live with feelings of hate and resentment. The support has been directed towards the survivors, since few want to work with the perpetrators in prison. These prisoners are locked in together with the haunting dreams and images of what they did. For many this makes it difficult to admit their crimes in the trials, which leads to even longer sentences and a circle of despair.

The staff of the Rwandan Correctional Services expressed that they had no tools to change the wellbeing of the detainees before they return to society. In the middle of 2013 Peaceful Heart Network was asked to do trainings in TTT to see if this could bring a change in the wellbeing of the detainees and improve cooperation in the prison.

Our colleague Murigo Veneranda has given trainings in all of the 14 prisons in Rwanda. The atmosphere between those who participated has changed, says the staff. They talk more and are more cooperative.

One detainee commented to Murigo:

"Is this method really good for me? It makes me want to talk about what I did in that time. Could you please ask the lawyer to come so I can tell my true story."

The social secretary of Nyamagabe prison, Dancille Muntu commented:

"Probably the best evaluation of this exercise is that the detainees keep doing it."

TTT in School

We have colleagues in Sweden who are teachers in a primary school. They introduced the tapping procedure in their classes as an exercise "to make the body and mind relax and to feel happy".

When they had been doing the tapping for some time they asked the pupils when they feel that it is useful to do tapping.

"When you have some spare time."
"When you are nervous, like when you are supposed to do a test."
"When you have "restless energy" in your legs."
"When something is scary.
"When you feel bad."
"When you want to be brave."

A similar exercise is done in by many school children in China up to grade four, it is called "eye sports gymnastics" and is presented as a natural method for making sure your eyes will be in good shape.

Integrate Locally!

Our work started in Rwanda and eastern Congo in 2007. Rwanda is a small country and eastern Congo a close neighbor, only few hours bus journey from Kigali, the Rwandan capital. Both places have need of trauma relief: Rwanda after the genocide in 1994 and eastern Congo because of the continuous conflict fueled by greed and desire for power that strongly affects the civil population. Also, what happens in one country affects the other.

We have been in Rwanda and eastern Congo many times, and our contact network has grown. We have reached thousands of people by working with local groups and organizations who have invited us to do trainings. Our networking skills and the experiences in Rwanda and Congo has taken us to countries such as Sierra Leone, Kenya, Chad, Uganda, South Sudan and lately also to India. The initiative often comes from somebody who has experienced and/or learned the technique and realized its potentials, read on our website or heard from others about our work and it's results.

Before starting to work in any location we have made good connections with the people or organization in each place, gaining trust through them. This allows a fairly new method, like TTT, to gain acceptance in a new environment.

"Nobody Offered Us Healing"

Gunilla:
Ahmat A was 17 when he was imprisoned the first time. He had heard on the radio that four "rebels" had been caught by the military and could be seen at the hospital. Ahmat, like many others, was curious to know what an "enemy" looked like, since there was so much talk about the threats against President Hissein Habré and his government. When Ahmat arrived at the hospital it turned out that the four "rebels" were exposed in the maternity ward on separate benches – dead and decapitated. The heads were faced staring towards those who came to see. Ahmat saw that they were young men. When looking at the faces he realized it could have been him, and started crying. The guards saw his grief and directly came down on him: *"Aha, you knew these rebels!"*

They grabbed him by force and Ahmat found himself imprisoned for rebellion in one of the infamous prisons of `N'djamena where torture was more a habit than an exception. His life of pain and opposition had begun leaving huge traces of traumas within him. It was to happen several times in his life even if he had no idea about that at the time and even if he never imagined himself as an activist or politician, circumstances made him one.

Many years later, in a conference about Human Security, Ahmat, now a parliamentarian, was asked why he didn't write a book about his experiences from the terrors of war. He responded:

"It gives me too much suffering to think about that time, I cannot think about the past without getting a severe headache and blurred vision."

A Canadian woman suggested: *"Why don't you ask Gunilla, she might be able to help you."*

"Really? That would be fantastic!"

We sat down and I explained how the procedure would be done.

"No problem", he said, closing his eyes, allowing his thoughts to move gently to the memories from the time of dictatorship.

The following day when our discussion group gathered again, Ahmat told his story of prosecution and suffering without any hesitation. We all listened amazed. He finished by saying:

"Today I dare to think about my past. I don't get that headache or blurred vision anymore. I could never imagine this would happen. I sincerely thank our sister from Sweden."

He added: *"Nobody ever offered healing to those of us suffering from trauma in Chad. Will you come?"*

Six months later we were in Chad doing TTT trainings, spreading ripples of healing.

The rough road to the Panzi Hospital in Bukavu, eastern Congo.

UNDERSTANDING STRESS

Taking a bicycle to a village workshop.

Mechanics of Stress and Trauma

Understanding the mechanics of stress is of great use when you want to offer TTT to somebody. Stress itself is not a bad thing. It is merely a response by our body and mind on perceived threat of any kind. It is meant to be a short-term condition that prepares and distributes our internal resources and soon declining when the threat is over. However, sometimes we get stuck in the stress state, which turns the healthy short-term reaction into long-term negative results.

The underlying mechanism is the collaboration of the two main parts of our nervous system; the sympathetic nervous system (SNS) and the parasympathetic nervous system (PSNS). The SNS is responsible for short term actions vital to survival, whereas the PSNS regulates long term actions vital to survival. In general, the SNS speeds up bodily processes and is responsible for the so called *fight or flight response* that most of us are familiar with. The PSNS on the other hand slows down bodily process and is mostly responsible for producing states of rest, or the *rest and digest response.*

When in a balanced state of mind, we actually move dynamically between SNS and PSNS activity, literally in every breath we take.

Alarm Mode

When you are in actual, or perceived, danger and need to prepare for fight or flight your body relocates all resources in an instant to provide maximum potential for survival. This is a whole system of pre-programmed responses belonging to the sympathetic nervous system:
- Blood is drawn away from your *digestive system* to your arms and legs, because running and/or defending yourself is – in case of an emergency – more important than digesting food. In the short term this gives you maximum power and ability to react. In the long run this could give you constipation or digestion problems.

- When the alarm center of the brain, controlled by the amygdala, hijacks your mind, blood is also drawn from your *frontal cortex*, the part of your thinking, logical and observing brain, located behind your forehead. This will leave you less oriented to thinking and more into reacting. In the short run this gives you fast reactions, whereas in the long run it will cause problems thinking straight, focusing and remembering.
- The stress hormone *adrenaline* affects your muscles. In the short term this provides peak power bursts. In the long run it will wear out your muscles creating a weakness.
- *Cortisol* is also released upon stress, and in the short run this will give you strength, but in the long run it will create a fragile internal landscape that opens up for more traumatic stress responses to be conditioned.
- You get *tunnel vision*, in the acute situation allowing you to focus on the most vital details of the current situation. In the longer perspective, you might have problems focusing on general issues of your life situation and those around you.
- Your *breathing* is elevated high in your chest, filling your muscles with the oxygen that in the short run will give you maximum leverage of power, and in the long run will cause problems falling asleep, since sleeping is something we don't do when we are in alert mode.

Fight, Flight, Freeze or Faint

There are four common reactions of our alarm center – the amygdala – when we are overwhelmed or threatened. Remember that none of these is a conscious choice, they are happening on an instinctual level and therefore they are sometimes called an *amygdala hijacking*.

Fight – *"I didn't even think, I just hit everything around me."*
Flight – *"I don't know what happened, when I came back to my senses I was running in the woods."*
Freeze – *"I don't know why, but I didn't protest, didn't move, didn't say a thing, I felt like it was happening to another person."*
Faint – *"I just passed out."*

Relax Mode

When we feel safe we find ourselves in the realm dominated by the PSNS, which is organized for taking long-term care of us, rest and digest. This is where eating and digestion starts working properly including resting, socializing, sex, sleep and recreation.

Breathing – the foundation of relaxation
Of all symptoms involved, there is one that you consciously can control, and by doing so, you will affect all the rest: your breathing. Your breathing is the connection between what your body does without you thinking about it, and what you can control by thinking about it. Breathing is the link between your two nervous systems, a gateway to relaxation. Breathing is what meditation, mindfulness, yoga, qigong and all holistic approaches have in common.

Re-Traumatization
There are methods for treating traumatic memories that require revisiting the feelings associated with these memories. For the nervous system of a person this can be the equivalent of experiencing the traumatic event again, actually reinforcing it. This is called re-traumatization and in our opinion, it should be avoided at all times. During all these years, we have never experienced the need to induce an abreaction to resolve a traumatic memory. This is one of the advantages of techniques like TTT: You do not need to talk about the event. You don't need to relive it – just connect ever so lightly to the unwanted emotion, while performing the technique.

Single Event Trauma
Single event traumas are isolated events perceived as traumatic, for example an accident, violence, rape, or witnessing either of these. You know what happened and when, maybe even what time it happened.

Summary Trauma
A summary trauma is an alarm state that the amygdala may have created from a number of, maybe even unrelated experiences. Examples of situations that can contribute to create this kind of traumatic stress are events that happen separated by a period of time, like challenging childhood, followed by an accident or loss later in life. Neither of these events were considered traumatic at the time, but the sum of them can start triggering traumatic stress responses. A summary trauma can also be the result of experiencing stress over a long period of time, for example being a single mother to a challenged or sick child.

The Snowball of Stress Responses
"Women who have been raped get traumatized, not only from the rape itself, but also from being pointed at by the others in the community. The shame is so bad that they get traumatized again. They often isolate themselves. A woman who gives birth after being raped will also suffer for that. And the children will be traumatized too since they are seen as offspring of the enemy."

From a workshop with women in Mumosho, Congo

Some traumatic stress reactions are related to our ways of rationalizing about what happened:

- Why did I survive and not everyone (guilt)?
- Why did I not make more resistance when I was violated (shame)?
- I am a monster, how could I be so violent (guilt)?

These thoughts can become a stress on their own, and since they are the result of an amygdala hijacking the rational answer is: You did this because, under pressure, your *fight or flight response* took over your rational brain and made you do what it thought was best at the moment for your survival.

Phobias and Allergies
Once a plant surfaces over the earth, it has already spent a lot of time building the necessary roots underneath.

Some stress symptoms can show up after more than 10 years and are often provoked into action by some other life-changing event such as a divorce, disease or even something positive like having children. Also, many phobias show up late in life after becoming a parent. A possible theory is that the brain, when taking the role of nurturing and protecting your genes, will scan back through every single memory of what to be careful about in order to protect your offspring, and sometimes this can lead to an unexplainable fear of flying or heights. Some allergies that show up late in life can be traced back to a traumatic experience, and resolved.

Trying TTT on these symptoms can prove very helpful.

The Encoding and Decoding of Trauma

"Sensory input to the brain, whether it comes from outside the body or from within, is transformed into an electrochemical signal, the language of our body."

Dr. Ronald A Ruden

There are three factors that need to be active for an event to be encoded and maintained by the brain as traumatic. This encoding will create a number of automatic triggers that can fire the same emotional distress and reactions (traumatic stress) long after the event is over (post).

The three factors are:

1. Inescapability
Perceiving an event as inescapable is subjective, it is about feeling trapped. This can for example mean being in an open space with nowhere to hide, or being caught by somebody or fearing to be killed.

2. A loss with personal meaning
The fear of losing something is a subjective perception. It could be a loss of reputation, power, status or social position, losing friends, family, home, integrity, body parts, property or money.

3. Current status of resilience to stress
Our current state of mind in relation to a stressful event plays a vital role for the encoding of trauma and is a neurological part of the process. Imagine that there is a bucket of resilience that can contain a number of related, or unrelated

stressful events during a lifetime. Once the bucket is full, any event can become the drop that makes the bucket spill over, allowing for encoding of trauma.

Once this event is experienced and encoded as traumatic, any of the stimuli present at the time of encoding (smells, sounds, images, objects, thoughts and other sensations) can trigger the emotional reaction as if the event is happening again.

The goal of treating trauma is to reset these responses – disconnecting the stimuli from the emotional reaction – allowing a larger space in the bucket of resilience.

Encoding

We use the model of encoding and decoding of Dr. Ronald Ruden. In this model, the neurological pathways during the encoding of a traumatic experience are the following:

1. All stimuli from our senses (sight, hearing, touch, smell and taste) enter the thalamus, our stimuli distribution center in the brain. The thalamus will sort these stimuli into two roads: one straight to the amygdala, for immediate trauma encoding, and one to our reflective mind (neocortex) for analysis and possible trauma encoding. Of all stimuli, smell is sent on an even faster track to the amygdala, bypassing the thalamus. This may be because it is our main – or most primitive – alarm channel.
2. Stimuli sent directly to the amygdala are usually those with high level of fear or threat such as a gun, knife or lion. Stimuli sent through the cortex are usually from the context of the event, and need some evaluation of importance, such as time of day, number of people present, noises, colors, type of situation or place.
3. All stimuli that are decided by the circuitry thalamus-amygdala-cortex to be associated with the traumatic experience are encoded in the "alarm checklist" of the amygdala, as fast synaptic connections (synaptic AMPA-receptors). These synaptic connections can associate and trigger an alarm extremely fast. This mechanism is most probably there to protect a person of getting into the same traumatizing situation again. The encoding of synaptic receptors is maintained with a neurological kind of glue that holds it unless something is done to release them.

Decoding
The prevailing theory is that these encoded synaptic receptors can be decoded by the following process:
1. **Activation** of the response mechanism that exposes the connection to emotions. This can be a stimuli triggering or thinking about the event(s). The activation level is measured subjectively with a SUD scale of 0–10.
2. **Decoding** of the response mechanisms by ungluing the encoded synaptic receptors.

This process is called de-potentiation. Our hypothesis is that applying Trauma Tapping in this situation, among other things, will contribute to creating Delta brainwaves (See: glossary) that trigger the production of chemicals and hormones that unglue the alarm receptors permanently.

Depotentiation and Meridians
When it comes to proving how Trauma Tapping and other sensory exposure therapies work there are two dominating approaches. That of depotentiation, as described above, and that of Body Meridians.

Body Meridians
The Trauma Tapping points coincide with a number of acupuncture points in Chinese medicine, which are aligned along what in this tradition are called body meridians, controlling the flow of energy (chi/qi) in our bodies. There is a theory that trauma is like a blocked or frozen memory in this energy flow that is unblocked by the action of tapping by stimulating the energy flow. The body meridians have not achieved acceptance in the western medical or science community, even if they have been used as a model of explanation for thousands of years in integrative medicine. This is the most common explanation among people using different versions of tapping when referred to as energy psychology.

Gunilla Hamne and Robert Ntabwoba conducting a workshop in Kiziguru, Rwanda.

Emotions, Thoughts and Behaviors

In our body and mind there is a constant dialogue emotions, thoughts and behaviors. We find it helpful to reflect on these interactions to understand how techniques like Trauma Tapping (sensory input) can alter emotions connected to memories or other signals to our senses.

Emotions

An emotion is technically a state of consciousness in which various internal sensations are experienced. Emotions can be produced by a thought, a memory or an external motivator triggering one of our five senses (sight, touch, sound, smell or taste). An emotion can often change our physical state by causing our body to react in different ways, controlling hormones and glands as well as the immune and defense systems.

An interesting aspect of our emotions is that it is only possible to feel most of them one at a time. It is hard to be happily angry or hysterically calm. When an emotion is strong you can switch from one feeling to another at the same strength: for example from scared to angry to laughter.

Thoughts

A thought may seem simple enough, but have you spent a thought thinking about how you actually create a thought? To create a thought you need to observe a thought or access a memory, which is associated to one or more of your five senses: an image (still or moving), a sound, a feeling, a smell or a taste. These memories are labeled by your rational brain, where language resides, into a cluster of information that holds a specific meaning to you. This is why the smell of roses in combination with wet feet can trigger the memory of a grandmother and being young, safe and happy for some people, and a feeling of hiding in the garden from a violent drunk parent for others. Ultimately, thoughts are our way of processing memories and giving them meaning.

Behaviors
Behaviors are things we do, whether by conscious choice or not. These include:
- **Bodily expressions** of our current state of mind, such as fidgeting or biting nails because we are restless
- **Bodily sympathetic actions**, such as sweating, high breathing, blushing, heartbeat
- **Compulsive behaviors**, such as smoking, drinking or doing something else compulsively and excessively

Positive Intentions
Instead of trying to find a negative label such as a *disorder* or *syndrome*, we take the perspective that every behavior has a positive intention. Find this intention and you will be able to redirect to another behavior if the current one isn't filling your needs.

An example of this is anxiety: If you feel anxiety there is a reason. The reason may not be relevant to anybody else, but for some reason it is relevant to your conscious or subconscious mind. And to feel it, you need to actively do something, consciously or subconsciously: Perceive a stimulus in the form of a sound, smell, sight, situation or feeling, or bring up the memory of one.

For example, the positive intention of
- **Anxiety** is to put you into alert mode to avoid a life threatening situation
- **Aggression** is to put you into a defense mode
- **Shame** is to alert you that something you just did might not be in your interest in the long run
- **Guilt** is to make you remember to avoid certain behaviors
- **Nightmares** are for your subconscious mind to "let the steam off" certain issues
- **Flashbacks** are to remind you to beware of a life-threatening situation
- **Problems sleeping** can intend to make sure you don't sleep through a life-threatening situation, or prompting you to resolve an emotional conflict.

All these behaviors are designed for short term use, in the sense that they are meant to put you in an alert state to save your life or remind you of something. If you stay on constant alert a longer time, chemicals will be produced in your body-system that are unfavorable. We propose that TTT can help the nervous system turn off this alarm, allowing a person to look for the positive intention, and addressing it in a more favorable way.

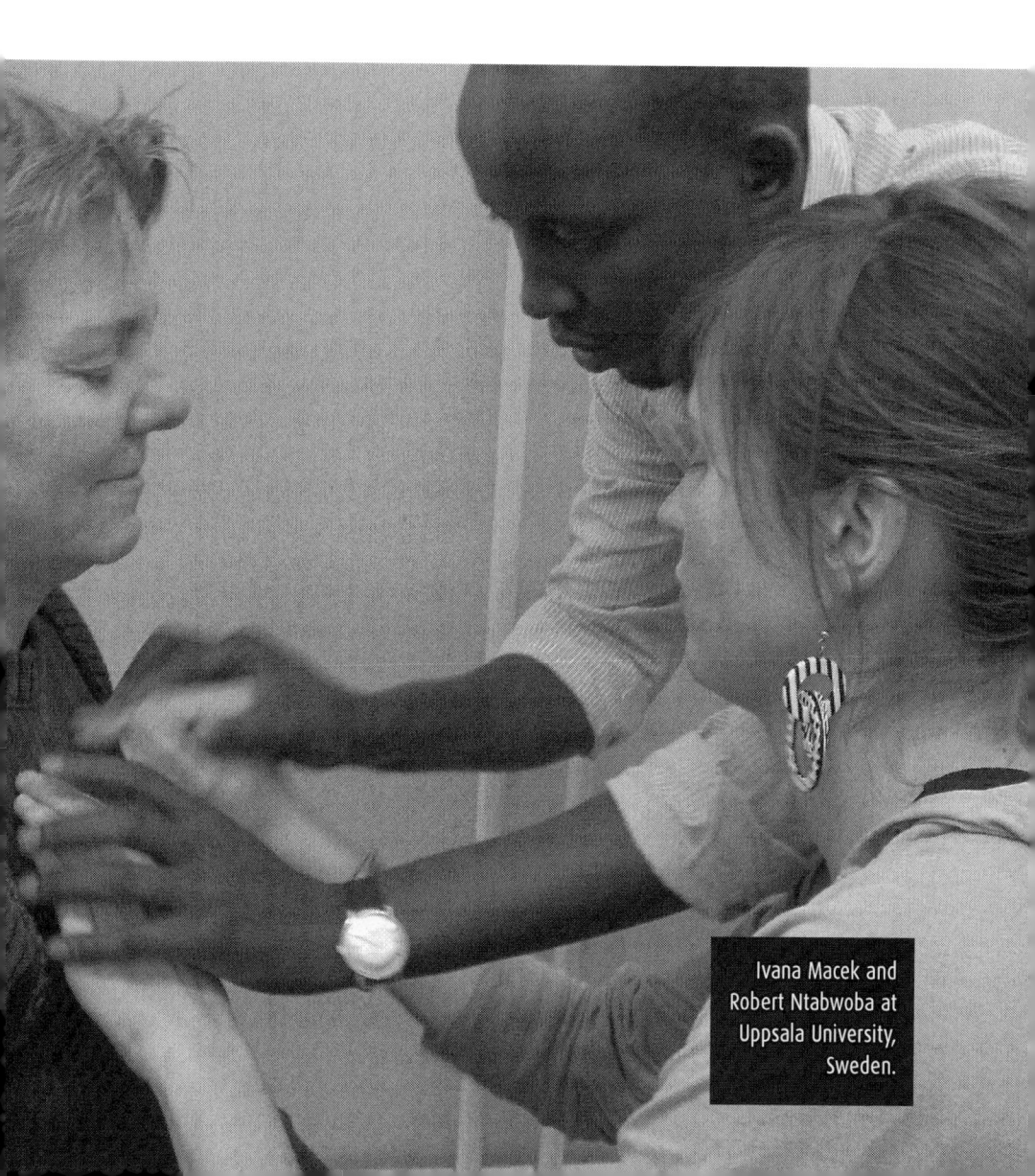

Ivana Macek and Robert Ntabwoba at Uppsala University, Sweden.

Germando Barathi from our TTT Center in Bukavu, Congo, with former child soldiers at BVES rehabilitation center.

Signs of Emotional and Traumatic Stress

Negative emotions like fear, rage, and anxiety all have a meaning. They carry a message so we can choose a better course of action, or avoid repeating old mistakes. They are like fire: it can warm you, protect you: or consume you.

As we cover in detail in the chapter about encoding stress, it is when we
- experience a situation that we perceive as inescapable and overwhelming
- stand to lose something of high personal importance such as our life, property, loved ones, or risk pain and humiliation
- already are in a fragile, or less resilient state of mind and body

that the situation can become encoded, conditioned into our nervous system as an alarm.

This conditioning will cause our nervous system to react as if the event is happening again long after the event is over and it will be triggered by any stimuli that reminds us of it, for example a sound, color, voice, smell or memory of some sort.

When we relive the event over and over again in this way we are experiencing a stress after (post) the traumatizing event.

The emotions that have been encoded to trigger with these memories can be de-encoded and released with psycho-sensory techniques like TTT. Some symptoms disappear after a single session – some may require two or more.

Three Types of Stress Symptoms

To understand which symptoms you can expect to disappear right away in a session, and which will need more time, we divide the symptoms into three types:

- The alarm is constantly on (persisting symptoms)
- The alarm is triggered from a conscious thought or dream (internal stimuli)
- The alarm is triggered by something you see, hear, feel, taste or smell (external stimuli)

Persisting Symptoms

Persistent symptoms are stress symptoms that remain on at all times, like an alarm that is sounding constantly.

These symptoms can disappear completely during a session of TTT and never return.

Triggered Symptoms

Triggered symptoms are the stress symptoms that show up when triggered by some kind of input, real or imagined, such as a sound, smell, feeling, sight or taste or the memory of one of these.

For these symptoms to be affected by a session, the person needs to be in touch with the feeling during the session. Treating somebody while they experience a symptom is a great way to succeed with this, whereas treating somebody for a symptom that isn't activated will have no effect on the symptom.

You could compare this to taking a shower: The treatment is like a shower that can wash away your symptoms, but if you leave your symptoms outside the shower, they cannot be washed away. At most you will be relaxed.

These are symptoms reported at our Trauma Tapping Centers in eastern Congo. They coincide with symptoms of PTSD in general.

- Nightmares or difficulty sleeping
- Flashbacks
- Anxiety
- Fear/Anger/Irritation
- Feeling of revenge
- Stomach ache
- Headache
- Other types of physical pain
- Palpitation (heartbeat)
- Difficulty breathing
- Tension in muscles
- Digestion problems
- Substance abuse
- Instability
- Forgetfulness
- Difficulty trusting anybody
- Dissociation from body
- Constantly feeling tired
- Hypertension
- Feeling weak
- Feeling worthless
- Being in a "bubble"
- A "jumble" in the head
- Difficult to concentrate
- Feeling isolated
- Not able to think about the future
- Reliving the past constantly
- Thoughts of suicide

Self-Medication and Suicide

A person suffering from post-traumatic stress may take to self-medication in the form of substance abuse, or even contemplate suicide as a solution. This can be a cycle that retriggers over and over, between periods of more normal behavior.

Drugs and alcohol can offer a feeling of detachment, which calms down the nervous system. However, the effect will wear off and there are side effects that are more dangerous to the person and their family or community in the long run.

Offering a conventional rehabilitation program for the substance abuse may not help, since the reason for self-medication, the trauma, is still there. Therefore we recommend that you view substance abuse as a possible symptom of traumatic stress, and offer a session of TTT.

In the same way, suicide can seem to be a logical alternative for a person who has tried everything. Going to a conventional therapy session to talk about a suicide attempt that was triggered by post-traumatic stress, involves a large risk of re-traumatization. Strangely enough, some sessions of TTT when the person is in contact with their negative emotions can be enough to offer the hope they need to see life as an alternative.

Surviving Sexual Abuse

If you, or somebody you know, have survived sexual abuse, regardless of whether it was verbal, physical or violent beyond imagination, TTT can help the healing process.

Sexual abuse, in any form, can be a traumatizing event in many ways. Before you read further, rest assured that it is possible to move on – and probably sooner than you think. We can say this from our experiences of working with women and men that have been sexually abused in the most unthinkable ways, and how they have healed. Never ask anybody to revisit the incident. It is not necessary. Treat the whole family if possible.

Scenario 1: Do I need to talk about it?

There is no need to talk about what happened for healing to take place, unless you specifically want to. You need to let go of all emotions connected to the memories of what happened to be able to move on. Do not allow the incident to continue taking place in your memories over and over again. One session of trauma tapping, when you are in contact with the emotions connected to the incident(s), is sometimes enough to open this path of healing.

Scenario 2: Can I let go of the shame?

Some feel shame for surviving rape when maybe others didn't, or shame for the act of sexual abuse in the eyes of society. Many ask themselves why they did not resist the abuse more, maybe they froze or went limp or dissociated into a mindset of "this isn't happening to me". All these reactions are normal. This is how our nervous system tries to protect us. If you had fought you may have been abused even more. Going limp and not fighting back happens when your brain takes over your system. It is not your fault. Rape is a crime to humanity, according to international law.

Scenario 3: Will I ever trust a man again?

Will you ever be able to trust a man or woman? The answer is yes. There are many good men and women, and once you can release the emotional responses to what happened, you will be able to tell the difference.

Scenario 4: Should I contact the authorities?

Should you file a report to the police? To be honest there is no correct answer to this. If the police are just and you can trust them to take you seriously the answer is yes. Every perpetrator should be prosecuted. However, if you feel that you may not benefit from reporting a crime, you must think about the following:
- Get a physical checkup right away. If you do this at a hospital don't wash first, in some countries they can secure DNA, which can be crucial to put the perpetrator in jail if possible.
- Test yourself for sexually transmitted diseases to protect yourself and your future partners.

Scenario 5: Should I talk about my experiences?

Holding on to a secret can be painful. If you have nobody to talk to, share it with the universe in your thoughts and use TTT when unwanted emotions take over.

Sexual Violence as a Weapon of War

The sexual violence against women in eastern Congo is rated among the worst kind of crimes against humanity in the modern world. Rape is used as a weapon of war between different armed groups, who fight to control the natural resources in the area. Rape is a cheap and efficient weapon. It destroys communities without using a single bullet. The rape is often committed in front of the husband and children, neighbors or other community members with the intention of humiliating them as much as possible.

The sexually abused women and girls are often stigmatized and sometimes even expelled from their communities. Many are physically so injured that they need extensive physical surgery to function normally.

If the woman or girl gets pregnant the child is considered a child of the enemy and not welcome. The men on their side feel worthless not having been able to defend their daughters and wives. The community is ruined and therefore easier to control for the rebels and armed groups, providing them access to the area.

This is not only done in Congo, rape and abductions have been weapons of war since warfare began when mankind settled down and could gather wealth to protect and fight for. However, it was after the war on the Balkans that rape was recognized as a weapon of war in modern times.

Children as Weapons of War

During the armed conflict in eastern Congo there has also been an extensive use of children as soldiers and sex slaves. Children are cheap, resilient and can easily be scared to do as they are told. The way they are used as child soldiers is among the worst you can imagine.

Sometimes they are brought to a medicine man and sprayed with "magic water" that will make them invincible to bullets, so they can be asked to run in front of the troops and take enemy fire, allowing the older soldiers to survive.

They are often abducted on their way to or from school, sometimes forced to kill their own family as young as 9–12 years. Many of them start as sex slaves and those who survive are given a gun when they are considered old enough, like Faida.

A Woman in Kiziguro
"I was raped by a young man several years ago. After that I avoided places where men would be, I would take another direction if I saw a man coming towards me in the road, no matter how old or young he was.

Since I got treated with TTT I feel like something new came into me, the change started the day of the training, but not completely. When I went on treating myself I really felt good, my problems gradually went away. Now I can greet men I meet, which was impossible earlier. I feel free from that trauma."

Faida – Former sex slave, child soldier and survivor
Gunilla:
Murhabazi Namegabe and his organization BVES, liberates and rehabilitates children who have been used as soldiers, porters and sex slaves in armed groups.

The girl I came to treat in Bukavu was 16 year old and her name was Faida. She had been kidnapped at the age of eleven by one of the armed rebel groups in eastern Congo. During four years she was used as a sex slave. One day she observed that the girls that carried guns were not raped, so she asked to be a soldier.

When Faida was liberated, she walked up to Murhabazi and looking at him with her dark determined eyes she asked him:

"*Monsieur Murhabazi, thank you for liberating me. But please tell me something: I have been raped by the whole platoon and I have learned to use a gun and how to kill. So tell me, who am I now?*"

Murhabazi stood wordless.

Faida was brought to the child soldier rehabilitation center for health check-ups and plans were made for her education since she, like most child soldiers, had lost many years of schooling while in the army. She moved into the house of a relative, an aunt high up on one of the hill side shanty towns outside Bukavu.

Very soon the aunt found Faida difficult to deal with since she easily got angry, screamed in her sleep because of nightmares and didn't manage to concentrate in school. She was annoyed and everybody around her as well. These were symptoms of trauma.

Murhabazi asked Faida if she wanted to try Trauma Tapping with me. Faida answered: "*Hakuna shida – No problem.*"

We decided to meet in the BVES office downtown Bukavu. For Faida this meant a long walk from where she lived. We went into one of the rooms and sat down side by side and I performed Trauma Tapping with her. She kept her eyes closed and did not open them when I was done. Finally Faida said: "*Now it's fine*" and opened her eyes.

We met two more times. The third time we met she smiled and said:

"*I have no more nightmares and I don't get angry anymore. My auntie is happy too. Do you know what I told the people in my neighborhood yesterday? I said: 'I am not the same person like before. I am like new. I have been re-formatted!'*"

Double Trauma for Anthony

Anthony was ten when he and his friend were abducted on their way home from school. He was to spend five years as a child soldier.

"They tied me up", Anthony tells, *"We didn't know where we were going."* Two days later his friend, just nine at the time, tried to escape. The rebel soldiers caught his friend and forced Anthony to beat him with a stick together with the soldiers.

"They forced me to beat him harder and harder, I didn't dare to refuse", says Anthony. *"My friend died there and then."*

The rebel leaders said *"We need you to be a strong child soldier."* They put Anthony and the other children through a brutal caning as an initiation, before taking them to Sudan to continue their training for child soldiers. They were constantly hungry and afraid and had to dig for roots and eat leaves to survive. After six months, Anthony had completed his "training" and was given a gun.

The rebel commanders thought Anthony was doing well, so he was sent with a group of soldiers into Uganda to steal food, medicines and other supplies needed. They plundered villages and if anyone resisted, Anthony and the other child soldiers were commanded to kill. At times they even had to kidnap children and take them back to the camp in Sudan.

During one of the looting missions in Uganda, he suddenly recognized where he was and made the decision to escape from the rebel army.

"I passed a farmer along the way working on his plot. When he looked up at me I recognized him from my village", Anthony says. *"I threw my gun down to show I didn't come to harm him, and to my big relief the man asked me to come with him to his house."*

From there Anthony was able to return to his family, where he learned that his father was dead. His mother was so happy to see Anthony alive. She had almost lost hope to see him again after all the years he had been gone. But she realized that they had to leave the village immediately: The rebels would come looking for Anthony since he had escaped – taking with him a valuable gun. They left with few things, running into the forest to hide. Only a few hours later, the rebels came. When they didn't find Anthony, they burnt down his family's house.

After escaping, the family got settled in a camp for internally displaced people (IDP). He went back to school and did his best to support his mother and the two remaining brothers. One day he was approached by a representative from an US based organization and invited to the US to go cycling in Ohio to raise money for a campaign to make people aware of what happened to children in war zones like Uganda. It sounded like a fantastic opportunity for Anthony.

Anthony turned out to be a very good cyclist. But instead of being gratified for his participation he ended up being used in a slave-like manner, working at the project manager's farm from early morning until late at night, taking care of and cleaning for the cows, the horses and the sheep, making fences, moving heavy stones, building sheds and clearing forest. He always had to do what the manager commanded him to do. He didn't get proper food and was not allowed to eat with the family, instead he had to sit eating alone in a store room.

Not only that, he also had to go around telling his story of being a child soldier over and over again at different events. The manager wanted him to tell the worst of his horrific experiences. Every time Anthony got re-traumatized and had difficulty to sleep because of nightmares. The manager kept saying that the organization supported the building of a school in Anthony's home village and that his family was getting money. But later on Anthony found out that no money was sent.

Anthony's rescue was learning how to use internet. He managed to get in contact with another former child soldier from Uganda, who was also in the US. She had written a book and had gotten established in American society. She encouraged Anthony to escape from the farm and promised to contact a lawyer who could take on his case.

In this way Anthony had to escape for the second time in his young life. He packed a plastic bag with some belongings and hid it under his bed. One Sunday when the family was in church, he said he felt sick and stayed behind in the house. When they had left he grabbed the plastic bag and ran.

Anthony says his experiences of humiliation and exploitation in the US were even worse than being a child soldier, because he was forced to be a soldier, but he came to the US by his own free will.

When Anthony had left the slave-like circumstances he got in contact with a Child Rights project I (Gunilla) have worked for. He told parts of his story and realizing he was traumatized I promised to visit him if I came to the US. So, after finishing a conference in Canada, I made a stopover in the city where Anthony was living on my way to New York. We met at a café in the central part of the city. Anthony told me his full story. He said he had difficulty sleeping and that his traumatic memories and fear kept haunting him. He was happy to hear that I could show and teach him a method that might ease his suffering.

Anthony didn't want to do the tapping in the café so we went out to find a more private place. Even though it was cold we decided to sit down on a bench in a Park. It was the most peaceful place we could find. The full moon of November was shining high up.

Here is what Anthony said a few days later over Skype:

"When you started the tapping I wondered really what that was all about. But I thought: 'Let me try.' And just after a moment I started feeling really, really good. It was great! I felt so relaxed and warm even though we were outside and it was kind of cold (laughter).

That night I slept like the day I was born. Like a baby! Before, I used to sleep only one or two hours at a time. I have a lot of medicines for sleeping, but they never gave me this kind of sleep. I could have slept even longer if my neighbor hadn't knocked on my door.

I love this tapping very much. I feel really, really peaceful when I do it. It is so cool! I have to say that this is the very best science. The one who found this treatment is very smart – he knows exactly how the body works.

Everybody can see how I have changed after this tapping. They say: 'What has happened to him? Why is he smiling all the time?' And I say: 'I'm finally being me again.' I hope that the sad me never comes again. And if he does – I will tap him away (laughter)."

Possession by Demons

"Save one person and you save the world"

Talmud

Beliefs in witchcraft are common in different parts of the world. Witchcraft and demons are used to clarify things that otherwise are not explainable. Bad spirits are said to take control over people when they have done something not acceptable for society. When possessed you are considered bad and dangerous. It's a curse. Therefore being seen as possessed by demons or crazy can, in Congo, be stigmatizing in itself. You become an outcast, and somebody may even try to kill you because you are frightening; a danger to them or the community.

One of the Trauma Tappers, Francoise, at our TTT center in Mumosho in Congo told about a related experience:

"I heard rumors about a young girl of 15, who was considered possessed by demons because she behaved strangely: She talked to herself, cried incessantly and screamed at night so the neighbors heard it. This girl had great difficulties with managing school and people were talking badly about her.

I met this girl on the road one day, so I went up to her and asked how she was doing. The girl seemed happy that somebody approached her and told me how haunted she felt by fearful images and dreams. She had probably been raped. That happens often here, but nobody will talk about it, since rape is associated with shame and even the risk of being excluded from the family and community.

I explained about the TTT center and the tapping and asked if she wanted to try a session. The girl said she would be happy to. Some days later she came to the center. I treated her and the girl seemed relaxed. I told her to continue tapping herself, and come back to the center. Next time I met her she looked different, her face was open and smiling. She said she felt as if a burden had been removed from her head."

First Time in 34 Years

"I have been like an orphan my whole life. My parents did not take care of me. I had to sleep outside in the banana plantation. My father was often drunk and would threaten to kill me. I saw how the other children got love and care and asked myself: 'How long will this continue?' When I was eleven years old I even thought of burning down our house so that others would understand our suffering.

Since my childhood I have suffered from migraine, pains, heart problems, panic attacks, fear and nightmares.

Often people trying to help me would make the mistake of believing that I listened to their comforting words. I pretended to do so, but deep inside I felt that nobody truly loved or cared for me. My daily prayer was: 'My God what is the meaning of living in this misery?' Death seemed better for me than this life full of problems.

In the beginning of the TTT training, I thought it was a waste of time since nobody had been able to solve my problems, to reach the dark room in my heart, in me.

I was wrong!

The Trauma Tapping has had a great impact on my life. Yesterday I was in despair, could love nobody and thought incessantly about suicide, today I have retrieved the joy of life! For the first time in 34 years I feel happy!

My husband said 'Tell me darling, what has happened to you, during our time together I have never seen you happy and smiling like now?' And he is right. I am different now. Our children are happy too. I know they have suffered from my sad state of mind.

I always thought that I was incapable of accomplishing anything, today I am restored. God bless you."

Deborah, Rwanda

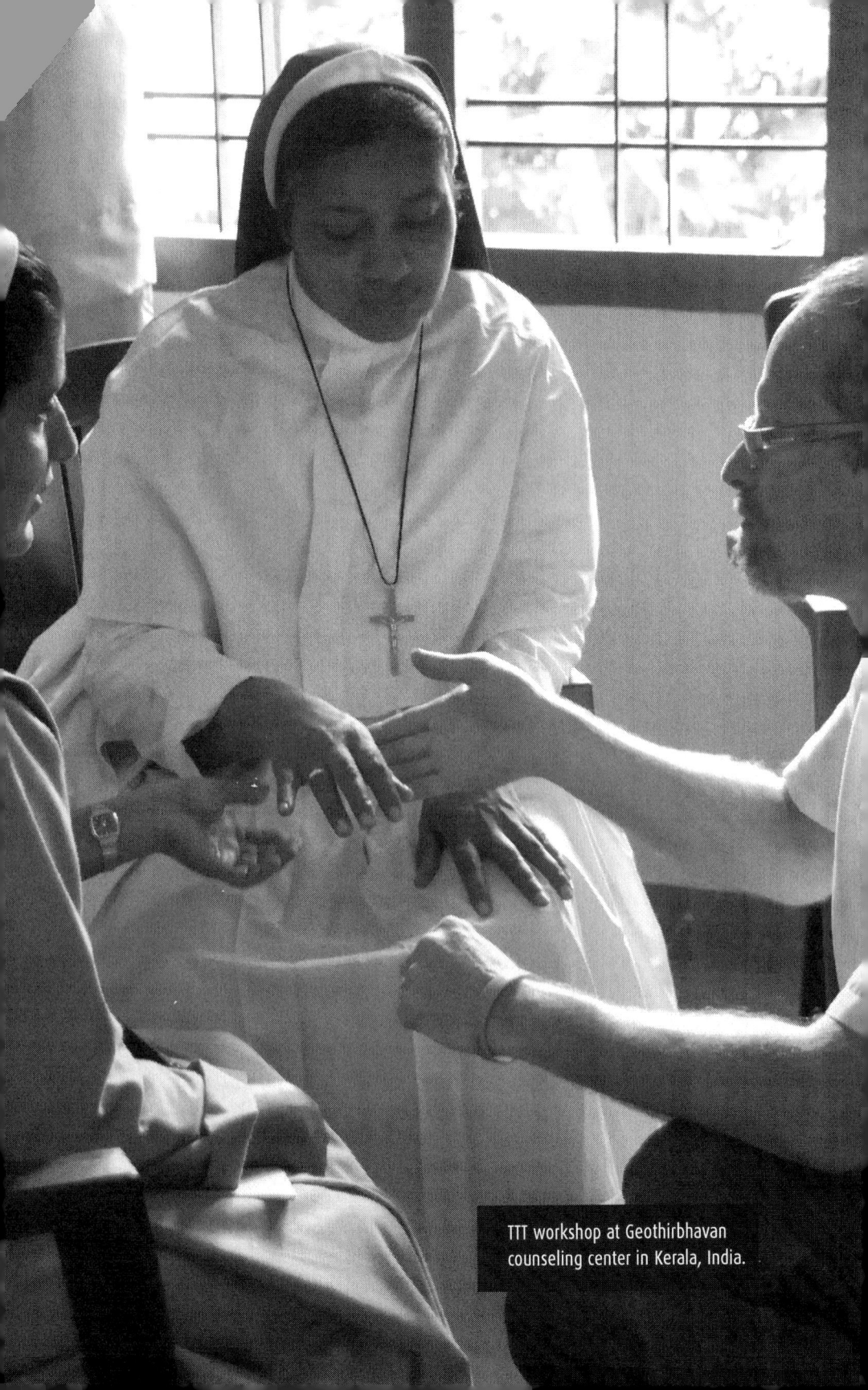

TTT workshop at Geothirbhavan counseling center in Kerala, India.

A General Mindset for Survival

Our mind is like a garden. We should water only the plants we wish to grow. Vital components in those who survive extreme situations such as war and abuse are:
- Their mindset
- Being connected to a higher spiritual value
- Caring for, or wanting to survive for the sake of somebody else

Healing is possible

When you accept that healing is possible, it becomes possible. Others have survived similar situations. With the right tools, you can do the same.

No matter what you have been told, these are facts:
- Post-traumatic stress is not chronic, you can heal from it.
- You cannot cure post-traumatic stress with medicines yet, but you can dampen symptoms temporarily.
- Traumatic experiences can heal fast.
- You can learn how to heal, even if there is not an expert available to help you.
- A traumatic stress reaction resides in a different part of your brain system than the rational and observing brain.

It can be helpful to be aware of our internal voice, because it can react in two general ways: One is to look for a reason for the traumatic experience by asking the following types of statements or questions:

"*This is typical!*"
"*Why does this always happen to me?*"
"*This is not fair!*"

Usually this type of thinking will not help, partly because there are no answers. We can train our inner voice to be proactive simply by taking care to start our reflective thoughts with words like what and how.

"What does this situation mean to me?"
"What can I do about it?"
"What can I learn from it?"
"What is the very first thing I can and need to do to move forward?"
"How can I find the strength to do this?"

Who would cope better than you?
Some people seem to face adversities better than others. What is it they do differently? By putting yourself in their shoes, you may find new perspectives.

Is there any other person, living, dead or imagined that would handle your current challenges better than you? Imagine, for example Jesus, Buddha, Mother Teresa, Nelson Mandela, Muhhamad or your favorite movie hero Pirate Captain Jack Sparrow perhaps (Yes, it's ok to include anybody here!) would respond to the trauma you experienced in your situation.

"What would they be doing differently?"
"Is there anything to stop you from doing the same?"
"If they were you, would trauma like you experienced stop them?"

What Is Your Vision of the Future?
It may be hard to appreciate how much your image of the future means for your ability to get there. A simple exercise can be asking yourself the following questions:

If you were to imagine yourself in the future, without your current challenges:

"What would be most different?"
"Who would be at your side?"
"Would anybody be less happy if your current challenges disappear?"
"In what ways would you be different from today physically or mentally?"

Also pay attention to how you allow yourself to paint your future in your mind. Are you imagining a goal you want to move away from?

"I want to stop…"
"I need to get out of…."
"I wish I didn't have…"

Or are you imagining a goal you want to move towards:

"I want to achieve …"
"I need to get…"
"I wish I had…"

Try both, and try to notice the difference in how they make you feel. Whatever empowers you is good. Generally speaking, positive goals are easier to focus on and achieve for most people as our brains do not distinguish negations, for example "*I don't want to smoke.*" will create an image of smoking, since the word "not" has no image. A positive goal that you want to move forward to is also more empowering than a negative goal that you want to move away from, for example "*I want to become happier*" is a more empowering goal than "*I don't want to be sad any more*".

Are there any limiting mindsets?
A limiting mindset is giving up trying to do something, because you have an illusion that it isn't possible. Examples of limiting mindsets are:

"It's no use, because…"
"I am not the kind of person that…"
"If I only had… it would be possible."

Remember now, this is in *your* mind, an illusion, something somebody may have told you that you may have accepted, and that stops you from thinking critically about positive possibilities for your future.

Ask yourself if you would like to lose this limiting belief or change it. What would be different?

Are you in the mindset of a victim or in that of a survivor?
Mindset is about how you view yourself. A victim is somebody who has been unjustly treated and needs help. A survivor is somebody who has been unjustly

treated and survived. Do you notice the difference? In the beginning of a survival process, it is natural to have the mind-set of a victim. When you move to the mindset of a survivor, you will be in charge of your destiny.

Post Traumatic Growth

When experiencing and living through the phases of trauma there is a potential for personal growth. This is called Post-Traumatic Growth. For this growth to occur it is necessary to let go of victimization. Instead the person finds her-/himself understanding and realizing things about themselves and others and the universe that would not have happened without the traumatic experience. This process becomes deeply meaningful for their lives and as a result their life quality is perceived as improved, as if they have gained something rather than lost, which might have been the first reaction.

Worldwide history offers a multitude of testimonies about individuals having changed their lives and thinking after a traumatically experienced event.

Caring in a Good Way

No matter how good your intentions are, caring in some ways can make a person feel worse than before.

Sympathizing can harm others
Be careful offering your sympathy to people who have suffered. Sometimes this will make things worse. Reading into your sympathy a person who has survived abuse and trauma may be reminded that they have experienced something terrible, and this can be very dis-empowering. Treat them like how you think they want to feel, not how you think they feel. Instead of sounding sorry for them, offer your help and support in a neutral voice, allowing them to calibrate their emotions.

Empathizing can harm you
To empathize with another person's trauma by imagining what they have been through is unnecessary and can put you at risk of developing a secondary trauma.

Compassion can empower
If you offer others your help in a way that empowers them, you will make them feel strong. This allows you to respect their pain and experience in a positive way. If you want to help a soldier, remember that his or her value system is built around self-sufficiency. Sympathy can be insulting and provoke aggressive responses, empathy too. Treat a survivor with respect, warmth and good humor.

We often say
"I cannot imagine how you feel, or what you have been through, but I am here for you and would like to offer my support if you wish to receive it."

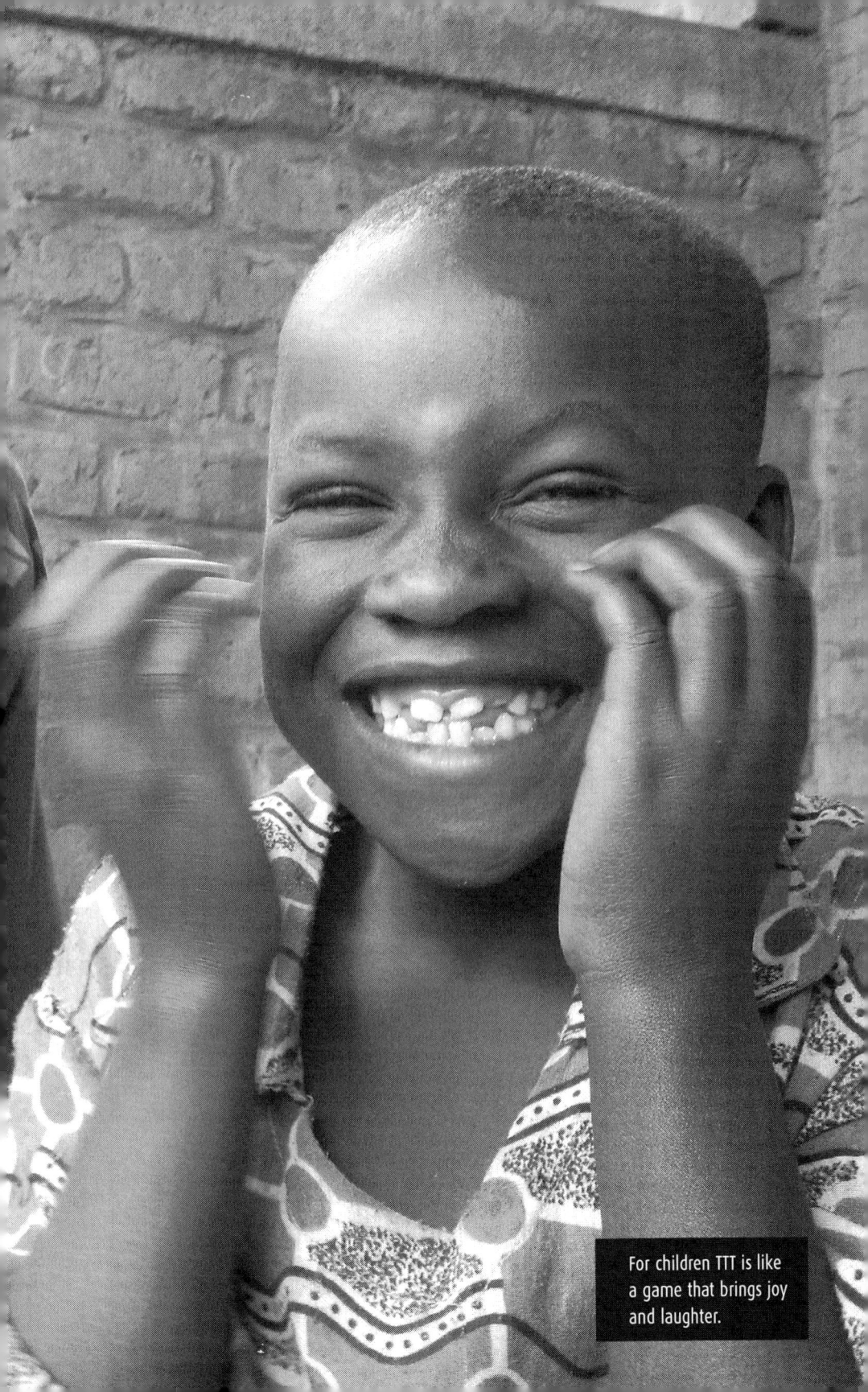

For children TTT is like a game that brings joy and laughter.

Picking up Emotions

Have you ever experienced a contagious mood where somebody else's joy or anguish seems to slip inside you, as if it was transferred?

In one part of our brain there are specialized neural cells, called mirror neurons, constantly mirroring the actions, movements and possible intentions of animals and people around us. This is believed to be part of what makes empathy possible, but also a part of how we can internalize other people's traumatic experiences when we are around them, with the risk of acquiring secondary, or vicarious trauma.

To avoid the kind of secondary trauma that can be transferred when you are working with traumatized people we use Trauma Tapping on ourselves and each other on a regular basis.

Positive Tapping

One way of protecting yourself is to tap on positive feelings to reinforce them. This is very simple: Anytime you experience a good feeling you simply do the tapping procedure and allow yourself to integrate the power of this good feeling.

Resilience to Trauma

Research shows that we can create a resistance to trauma – resilience.

Resilience is the ability to bounce back from a traumatic incident, allowing it to glide off our nervous system leaving it as a memory, without attached emotional responses. Research also indicates that it may be possible for us to train ourselves to avoid the emotional response after experiencing a traumatic event.

Resilience is also about creating mental and physical conditions in which traumatic overwhelming responses are less likely to happen. Both mental and physical preparedness is important when we wish to avoid a traumatic reaction.

Be mentally prepared for the unexpected

When something unexpected and overwhelming happens for which we are totally unprepared, we usually go into shock, a defense mechanism like: *"I have no idea how to handle this, so I'm not moving until I do know."* In some situations this is useful, in some not.

After shock many of us pass into disbelief: *"This can't be true."* The function of this stage remains a mystery, but maybe it is the brain's reaction to things not being the way they should – according to our previous knowledge and perceptions. Once we pass through the disbelief phase we move into the stage of acceptance *"This is actually happening."* followed by action *"What can I do about it?"*.

When you are mentally prepared for the unexpected, you are able to pass faster through these stages. When you know at least some options for action you will be able to choose one faster. Falling down to the floor when you hear gunfire is often a useful action. Knowing this and being prepared to do so speeds up your reactions. Knowing how to stop a bleeding or how to give mouth to mouth resuscitation for somebody who has been saved from drowning allows these actions to happen faster. Your library of possible actions is, in a way, a resilience factor.

Be physically fit and stress free

If your body is in good condition and low on stress hormones, this will give you a much better chance of not becoming traumatized.

Exercise regularly

Find some way to exercise regularly, no matter how little. By doing so you clean out the potentially harmful chemicals of the body, boost the immune system and bring oxygen to your brain. Research shows that exercising ever so little can make a big difference:
- A daily ten minute Do-In self massage
- Five minutes of push-ups
- Take the stairs instead of the elevator
- Carry the bags for somebody
- Walk or bicycle instead of taking a motor transportation
- Dance as often as you can

Meditate regularly

Make sure you consciously allow your mind to calm down in some way regularly, regardless of how little. Any of the following mental exercises will lower your stress levels and increase your resilience more than you may think. You can increase your resilience by doing some of these things.
- Allow yourself a moment of daydreaming
- Listen to your inner voice/your higher self/God
- Call somebody you love or like
- Read a book
- Watch a sunset, a lake, a tree, a flower, a bird
- Watch a movie
- Sing and/or play music
- Hug or touch a dear person
- Learn a sun salutation (surya namaskar) of any yoga tradition
- Take three Alpha-Theta slow breaths at any time
- Do Trauma Tapping on a positive emotion

Eat smart

Your body and mind are similar to a car in terms of needs: If you fill the tank with good fuel, it will function well. Again, there are some very simple rules that can make the difference between life and death in the long run. They are mainly about avoiding excess:

- Be moderate on alcohol – it stops your chemical system from rebounding properly.
- Be moderate on sugar and salt – they will mess up your energy resources.
- Avoid processed foods. Eat nuts, seeds, fruits and vegetables.
- Be moderate on foods with white processed flour in it such as white bread.

Factors that contribute to resilience include:
- Close relationships with family and friends
- A positive view of yourself and confidence in your strengths and abilities
- The ability to manage strong feelings and impulses
- Good problem-solving and communication skills
- Feeling in control
- Seeking help and resources
- Seeing yourself as resilient (rather than as a victim)
- Coping with stress in healthy ways and avoiding harmful coping strategies, such as substance abuse
- Helping others
- Finding positive meaning and purpose in your life despite difficult or traumatic events

An Overview of PTSD Treatments

Most approaches to treating or subduing the effects of post-traumatic stress can be divided into three categories:
- Psychotherapeutic approaches
- Medication
- Body-Mind oriented techniques such as TTT

Our reason for staying with TTT up to now is that we have not found a more efficient method that fits into our vision of passing it on as a first aid method empowering every survivor on an individual level, regardless of background, education or experience. Here is an overview of other frequently used methods:

Psychotherapeutic Approaches
There are different psychotherapeutic approaches to treating traumatic stress. One of the most common methods is Cognitive Behavioral Therapy (CBT), which is an action oriented method built on desensitizing responses through systematic behavioral training. Although there is a success rate there is also a risk of re-traumatization, since the therapy involves activating the unwanted emotional responses.

Medication
Using medication for traumatic stress can be like putting a lid on a jar full of bees, they will be kept away until the lid is taken off again. Sometimes medication is necessary to make life manageable during a transition period, but it is not an ideal long term solution.

Antipsychotics during a short period can relieve severe anxiety related problems, such as difficulty sleeping, emotional outbursts or aberrant and intrusive thought patterns.

Antidepressants can help symptoms of depression and anxiety. They also help to reduce sleeping problems and improve concentration. The selective serotonin reuptake inhibitor (SSRI) medications sertraline (Zoloft) and paroxetine (Paxil) are approved by the Food and Drug Administration (FDA) for the treatment of PTSD.

The body gets used to these medications and cutting some of them short without consulting your health provider can cause more trouble than taking them. Few medications are designed for long-term use. Always consult a trained medical expert regarding decisions around medication.

Body-mind oriented techniques

Other techniques in the same category as Trauma Tapping.

Eye movement techniques are an evolution from part of the protocol of early tapping techniques. Eye Movement Desensitization and Reprocessing (EMDR) was developed by Francine Shapiro and has undergone extensive clinical testing and is now approved and endorsed by for example American Psychological Association. Integral Eye Movement Technique (IEMT) is a later technique claiming a more precise methodology, originally developed by Andrew T. Austin based on the work by Connirae and Steve Andreas. Other eye movement interventions include Rapid Eye Therapy (RET), the creation of Renae Johnson, and Brain Spotting, the procedure developed by David Grand.

Havening is a technique designed by Dr. Ronald A Ruden after his research into how post-traumatic stress is encoded and can be decoded. The technique consists of systematic stroking of parts of the upper body after activating an unwanted emotional response in combination with eye movements, spoken phrases and humming. The mechanisms involved are those described as depotentiation in this book. We use Havening and find it powerful.

Tension or Trauma Releasing Exercises (TRE) is a technique allowing the body to release tension and emotions from traumatic experiences through a physically induced vibration of muscular tissue.

Meditation and Mindfulness are basically two ends of the same stick. Meditation has been part of Buddhist and Hindu spiritual practices in the East for over 5000 years as ways of body and mind control and lowering of anxiety. Jon Kabat-Zinn was a student of Zen Master Seung Sahn. His studies and practice of yoga and meditation led him to integrate these techniques with those of Western science. He has successfully introduced mindfulness meditation in the

West, which has been proved to help people cope with stress, anxiety, pain and illness.

Yoga, Qigong and physical exercise have been clinically tested and proven to improve life quality for people diagnosed with posttraumatic stress.

Other language oriented techniques

All of these techniques are powerful tools, and have a language-dependency in common. When language isn't an issue we use them, often in combination with TTT.

Hypnotherapy is a technique that can reach the emotions of the body through the mind. It is a naturally relaxed and focused state of mind that can be induced with the aid of simple techniques. In this state of mind we are more capable of solving and balancing emotions and conditioned responses, such as post-traumatic stress. Hypnosis in itself is just a state of mind, so the therapeutic effect of being in this state of mind will depend completely on what kind of techniques that are used while in hypnosis.

Neurolinguistic Programming (NLP) is an approach to communication, personal development and change created by Richard Bandler and John Grinder in the 1970s. The technique is based on the assumption that there is a connection between our neurological processes (neuro), our use of language (linguistics) and our behavioral patterns (programming). We use NLP techniques, the somatic poem being a good example of this.

Clean Language is a method for eliciting a client's metaphors and inducing positive change, developed by David Grove during over 30 years consisting of a small number of specifically worded questions. We find it efficient, and easy to learn, teach and use.

Bukavu, by Lake Kivu, Congo.

ADDITIONAL TECHNIQUES

Emotional Body-Techniques

Tapping may look like a joke or something strange to many, but in most cultures there are similar gestures. Let us just give some examples.

In Swedish there is an expression *"Ta sig för pannan"* which means to put the palm on the forehead – an expression of shock. When placing the hand on the forehead one touches some of the points used in Trauma Tapping. Holding the forehead – and around the head – when somebody is sick, distressed or feeling dizzy can be found in many healing traditions; be it in the Amazon forest, in cities of Europe or African villages.

Holding the hands in front of the eyes and the face, massaging the face, is another way we without thinking about it will help ourselves to lower the stress level.

In the Muslim tradition of Muharram, the ceremony of grief, clapping the chest is done when bringing up memories of lost ones. This procedure can also be found in for example Africa, sometimes in the form of a more caressing of the chest of oneself or somebody.

When feeling nervous or distressed you can see people wringing their hands. Others will hold their arms around themselves or let themselves be hugged by somebody.

When having a headache or being distressed by heavy thoughts many tend to massage their temples.

Be on the lookout for these ways of using the body to heal distress and you will find even more.

Also the method called Havening (which will be briefly mentioned later) is based on these gestures.

When you feel happy your body produces the hormones *serotonin* and *dopamine*, and the body reaction is to smile. Did you know that you can induce this process by putting a pen in your mouth for a couple of minutes – forcing a smile that will trigger your dopamine system?

High shoulders and *high breathing* are results of being in *fight or flight response*. If you are calm, try pulling up your shoulders and breathing high and fast, and see what happens to your mind.

Low breathing is the result of being calm under the influence of the parasympathetic nervous system. Next time you experience stress of some kind you may want to try *alpha-theta breathing*: simply take a deep breath through your nose and while counting to 3, then breathe out slooooowly through tight, pursed lips and count to 6.

Crown Pull

During a traumatic stress response, blood is normally drawn away from the prefrontal cortex – the center for logical thinking – residing behind your forehead. A Crown Pull will massage this part of the head, bringing the blood flow back and clearing the mind. We sometimes add a Crown Pull after the karate point, before starting to tap on the forehead.

Crown pull for somebody else
Put your fingers on the temples and use your thumbs to pull from the center of the forehead to the sides with a fair amount of pressure, around three times.

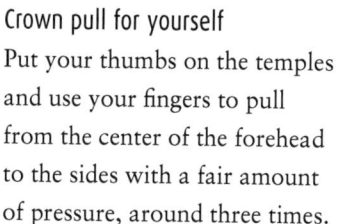

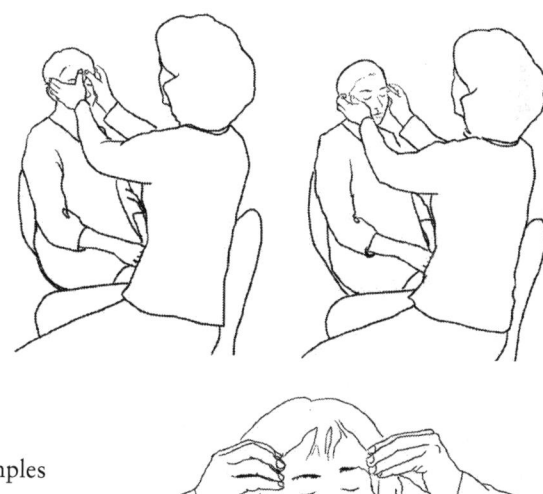

Crown pull for yourself
Put your thumbs on the temples and use your fingers to pull from the center of the forehead to the sides with a fair amount of pressure, around three times.

Resolving Yesterday - First Aid for Stress and Trauma with TTT

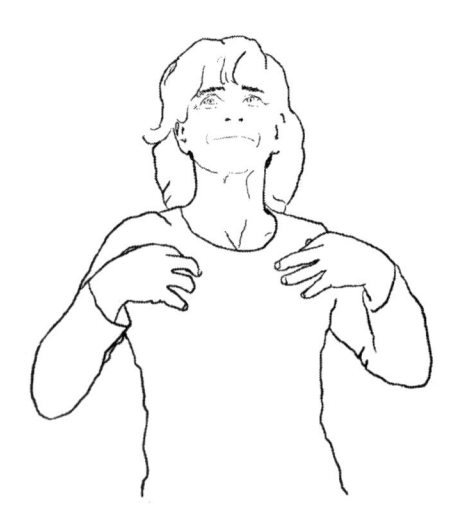

Gorilla Tapping Relief

If you forget all the other points, at least remember the tapping of the chest. The chest is a very potent area for tapping wellbeing into the nervous system. The chest is where we instinctively touch a child or a pet.

Also, when we feel insecure and anxious we tend to fold our shoulders forward to protect the chest, this sensitive area of the heart, the lungs and feelings. Just tapping the chest can resolve a lot of tension.

We call this Gorilla tapping since most people know how the gorillas do it, especially when we work near the mountain gorillas in the Virunga Mountains on the border between Rwanda, Uganda and Congo and the lowland gorillas in the national park of Kahuzi Biega in South Kivu in Congo. The gorillas tap the chest to show that they are fine. The sound is spectacular, like a talking drum.

"I often use the Gorilla tapping when I feel my emotions running in situations when I need to be calm and centered. I am kind of sensitive. Like during the ceremony of World's Children's Prize that I have worked with for many years. We give a prize to people who have done extraordinary things for the rights of the child somewhere in the world. The ceremony is often very emotional. But I am the coordinator and need to stay alert. So when emotions start running inside I turn to Gorilla tapping. Very slowly and without attracting attention. And the tears withdraw."

Gunilla Hamne

Soothing Head Holding

To finalize a tapping session or when somebody is too agitated to appreciate tapping, a good way of relaxing the mind is to hold the hands still and firm around the head. This position is traditionally used in many cultures when somebody is sick, has a headache or is feeling unstable.

Place one hand with the palm on the front of the head and the other hand at the back of the head with the little finger under the base of the skull and the rest of the hand on the rounded part on the back of the head just above the neck.

Stay like that for some five minutes or until the person feels calm. A slight pressure-release movement with the hands can be soothing. Release very slowly.

The head holding not only calms down the nervous system, it seems also to process emotions and reactions of stress. It also makes the person feel safe and held.

You can also administer the head holding to yourself. There is whole concept called TAT – Tapas Acupressure Technique – using head holding techniques. For more information see www.tatlife.com

Alpha-Theta Breathing

Taking control of your breathing and making sure that you breathe out slower than you breathe in will take you from a situation where you may be in the sympathetic nervous system (fight or flight response) into the parasympathetic nervous system where you are calmer. Two breaths are enough, and three can be magical.

1. Take a quick deep breath through your nose.
2. Hold your breath for a couple of seconds. Notice what it feels like.
3. Let your breath out through loose lips, like a deep sigh. Allow your shoulders to fall. Notice the feeling just after letting your breath out, before you start to breathe in.
4. Repeat 2–3 times.

This breathing is very efficient and will have a calming effect on its own. It is also the breathing we teach between both rounds of tapping and after. The names Alpha and Theta refer to our brainwaves, where Theta is a calmer brainwave than Alpha, and the exercise serves in going from one to the other.

Balancing the Brain

This exercise originates from the Thought Field Therapy (TFT) – protocol of tapping. It is often called the *9 gamut exercise*. In TTT it has been removed because people got confused with the eye rolling and some thought it looked "crazy" resulting in the rest of the treatment being forgotten. But it is a good exercise that seems to stimulate the brain and enhance the connections between the left and the right hemisphere. Each separate eye movement in this exercise stimulates a different activity in the brain.

Perform the following actions while tapping on the upside of your hand, on the point between the middle hand bones leading to the little finger and the ring finger.

1. Eyes closed
2. Eyes open
3. Look deep down right (head steady)
4. Look deep down left (head steady)
5. Look high up left
6. Look high up right
7. Roll eyes in a circle
8. Roll eyes opposite direction
9. Hum a tune for 5–10 seconds
10. Count down from 10 to zero
11. Hum a tune again
12. Close eyes and relax
13. Observe/notice any change

Do-in Self Massage

This is a self-massage that we often teach groups in connection with TTT trainings. It takes 10–15 minutes.

Do-in is Japanese and means to guide or lead people with physical/emotional suffering to find the path to clarity.

Giving your body this attention will benefit your health, increase blood circulation and make you feel more awake. While doing the exercise send grateful thoughts to your body, thanking it for being there for you. Gratitude is good medicine.

Stand with your feet shoulder width apart, arms hanging loose along the sides of the body.

Take some deep breaths and notice how the body feels.

1. Massage the palm with the thumb thoroughly.
2. Massage the backside of the hand by passing the thumb in the valley between the bones leading to the knuckles. Change hand and repeat from 1.
3. Place one hand under the navel, rotate and twist each finger separately. Do the same with the other hand.
4. Clap or tap all over the head.
5. Place the thumbs on the temples and with the fingers somewhat curled "open" the forehead, i.e. pull the fingers from the middle to the sides three or more times.
6. With the left hand, clap on the inside of the right arm downwards, and on the outside going up. Do the same on the other arm.
7. Pull/drag with your index fingers behind the ear, along the side of the scull bone.
8. Squeeze the eyebrows between the thumb and the index finger, starting above the nose.
9. Press with the fingertips along the roots of your upper row of teeth. Do the same with the lower row of teeth.
10. Massage the whole face.
11. Pull your ears, stretching them as much as possible in all directions.
12. Stroke the throat, giving the thyroid gland massage.
13. Squeeze the muscles of the neck; first with one hand then the other.

14. Clap the left shoulder with the rights hand, supporting the elbow with the other hand, reaching down as far as possible. Change side.
15. Tap the chest with your fingertips or clap with the palms – like the Gorilla tapping.
16. Clap under the arm, from the armpit down to the hip.
17. Massage the belly by softly circulating the palms clockwise.
18. Bend forward and clap the back, reach as high up as possible.
19. Clap the hips and the bottom.
20. Clap along the legs on the outside going down and on the inside going up.
21. Take your kneecaps in your hands and make a circular movement, like dancing or twisting. Both directions.
22. Walk on the spot – or around if you have space – first on the toes, then on the heels, then on the outside of the feet and finally on the inside of the feet.
23. Stand still with eyes closed for a while, take some deep breaths and notice if there is any difference in how the body feels.

Do-In training in a refugee camp outside Goma in Congo.

Aggression Blow-Out

Blow-Out is an extremely useful and fast technique for quickly rebalancing your nervous system if it is wound up in strong emotions of anger, aggression, anxiety or fear. It is used by special military troops before and after operations, and is just as useful for anybody from an angry kid to a city driver caught in an aggressive reaction. It is a much more efficient calming technique than counting to ten when your *fight or flight response* is activated, and will clear your head, clear out carbon dioxides and energize your system.

1. Lift both hands over your head and clench your fists hard.
2. Take a deep breath and hold it.
3. Pull down real fast and blow out the air with your elbows pointing down (think Karate).
4. Repeat three times.

Energizing Power Posing

Power posing is a technique built on the research showing that the body can influence our thoughts and hormones just like our thoughts and hormones can influence our body postures. One of the most viewed www.Ted.com talks is called *Your Body Language Shapes Who You Are* by social psychologist Amy Cuddy. It shows how power posing by standing in a posture of confidence, even when we don't feel confident, can affect testosterone and cortisol levels in the brain.

The simplest form of power posing is the gesture of success that has been proven to be the same for all humans, regardless of culture – and even by a blind person with no visual influence from others.

Stand with your hands out from your body as if greeting the sun, and the palms of your hands upwards. Lift your chin as if looking at the sun.

If you stand like this for five minutes a day, it will change your levels of testosterone and cortisol, making you appear and feel more confident and at ease.

As you may note, we have made this technique the first step of the Somatic Poem we use as a setup for group trainings with TTT.

The Pathfinder Cards

The Pathfinder Cards are an image based coaching method that came up during a long email conversation with the social activist, martial arts instructor and poet Gerard Osenele Ukpan in London. We were exploring non-verbal coaching that anybody can use on their own, to find a way out from an emotionally stuck position.

The Pathfinder Cards are based on metaphorical healing methods, where a person is prompted to translate their challenge to something visual.

This is the concept:
1. Think of a challenge in your life.
2. Pick a card at random (close your eyes and put your finger on one).
3. Allow your mind to reflect freely on possible relations between that image and your challenge.
4. Pick another card and repeat.

Continue until you can sense a new direction of thoughts or emotions.

The next page has a sample of the images. You can download them from our website as a pdf and as an application.

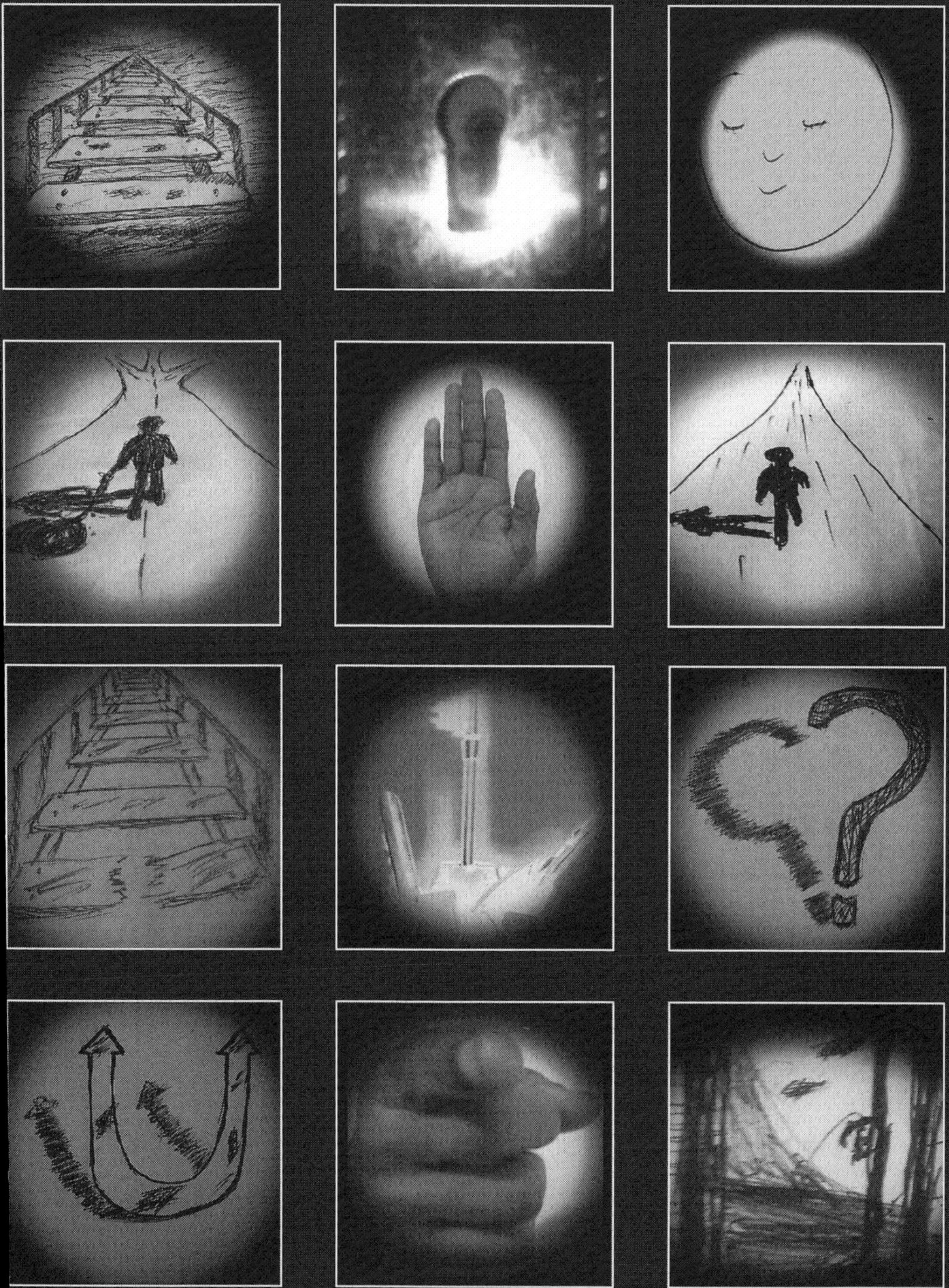

Roadside view over Rusizi, on the border between Rwanda and Congo.

PEACEFUL HEART NETWORK

At a workshop in Cyuve, Rwanda.

Our Vision

Working with TTT in the Peaceful Heart Network over these years we have seen that emotional and post-traumatic stress can be healed. We know it can be done simply, in large groups, with severe traumas and at very low cost. We know that it can be done with a first aid method that literally resides in the hands of every human, and that can be passed on from anyone to everyone.

We would like this method to be investigated, scrutinized, tested and scientifically proven, but until this happens, we want every person suffering from nightmares, flashbacks, sleeplessness, loss of hope, outbursts of aggression, indigestion and all the other symptoms of post traumatic stress to have a chance to heal and move on.

We want everybody working with children to know TTT and implement it to lower the impact of traumatic events in childhood – when so many of our fears in life become unnecessarily imprinted when they can be avoided.

We would like the Red Cross, refugee camps, prison systems and every other organization involved in teaching First Aid methods, or taking care of traumatized people, to know about it and incorporate it next to mouth to mouth resuscitation and the Heimlich maneuver as a First Aid for emotional stress.

If you feel like helping us in this, let everybody know. Call us for a workshop. Download the materials. Pass them on. World Peace Starts In You.

Building Peace

Imam Ashafa and Pastor Wuye used to be enemies, the former belonging to a Muslim militia and the latter being a member of a Christian one in the north of Nigeria. As a young man, Muhammad Ashafa followed the family vocation and became an Imam. He joined a fanatical Islamic group committed to completely Islamizing the north of Nigeria and chasing away all non-Muslims from the region inciting great violence in northern Nigeria. This resulted in the Christians creating their own counter organization led by Pastor James Wuye, who had always been fascinated by battle and war games involved in militant Christian activities. At one point they realized the futility in being enemies and started working together to build a method to assist conflicting groups of people and communities to build peace.

Pastor Wuye lost his arm in the fighting: *"I lost it because we didn't know how to talk"*, he often says, to show that he finds part of the responsibility for the arm being lost in his own actions.

Thanks to the documentaries produced by Alan Channer, their work is known worldwide, and they are invited all over the globe to facilitate reconciliation and peace building processes.

From their own experience in Nigeria and from other parts of the world, Imam Ashafa and Pastor Wuye have realized that a method for healing trauma that can easily be spread to many is needed for creating peace in conflicting societies.

We met again during trainings for Peace Building and Reconciliation between different ethnic and religious groups in Kenya. During the workshop Imam Ashafa introduced TTT to the 50 delegates: *"This Trauma Tapping is a new and universal method. The method crosses over all the borders of spiritual traditions, nationality, gender and race. And it is so simple. We need such an approach to help those who are traumatized and to be able to build long lasting peace. I encourage you to consider this seriously."*

Almost War

Emmily Korir belongs to the Kalenjin tribe in western Kenya. On occasions there have been clashes between Kalenjin and the other tribes in the area especially the Kikuyus and the Luos. The conflicts have grown out of different views on how to share land resources, conflicting interests and lack of communication.

Just days before our TTT workshop, Emmily almost started a small war in the town of Eldoret. She had been pushed over by a Kikuyu trader in the market of downtown Eldoret. She was injured and got so angry that she started shouting for the Kalenjins around to help her take revenge. A mob built up fast, ready to start a fight. If the police in the vicinity hadn't fired warning shots it would probably have gotten out of hand. This is what can happen when there is a lot of unresolved trauma in a society.

Emmily was still mad about this situation, so we used this to demonstrate a Trauma Tapping session, and to help her feel better about it. When Emmily experienced the radical change of her emotional reactions she was surprised.

"Before the treatment, just hearing the Kikuyo language could make me sick, so deep was my hate." Emmily explained. Today she is one of our most devoted Trauma Tappers. Two days after the workshop I got this message from Emmily:

"Thank you for educating us in Trauma Tapping. I did it with 32 women yesterday, and we are very happy about it. They said they would go home and do it with family and neighbors. Tomorrow I will do it with single mothers. The school is closed, but in January I will do it with the children. For youth I will do it next week when we have a Youth Forum. Actually I also did it with a passenger who was in the same bus yesterday."

Hanging around in Rwanda.

To Ease Suffering and Prevent Violence

"By helping people recognize the role of anxiety in bad personal and collective decisions and habits, and by giving them tools to reduce the anxious response in their bodies, they can make better choices. And that is a substantial contribution to a better life and a better world."

Dr. David Feinstein

The Holocaust, conflicts in Iraq, Afghanistan and the former Yugoslavia – every war is in one way or the other traumatic for the world community. They portray, too graphically, the price we will pay as a society if we stay in the cycle of trauma.

Traumatized people have difficulties in living in peace with themselves and others. In some instances trauma creates violence when the pain inside is acted out. In areas where memories of war are fresh and both sides of the conflict are living together, the process of reconciliation depends on each individual's peace within their heart and mind. On a national level we see countries being in conflict or war because of unresolved traumas, often transferred from one generation to the next. When the trauma is relieved, individuals, families, communities and nations can make better choices and decisions.

In the US alone there are 300 000 traumatized ex-combatants from the wars of Vietnam, Iraq and Afghanistan. Many of them have become homeless, out of work and/or violent because of their traumas. Each day one ex-soldier commits suicide and so far more soldiers have died from their own hand than in combat. Imagine how this affects not only them, but also their families and the society!

Our motto is *to ease suffering and prevent violence*. It is a great suffering to be traumatized – a suffering that affects not only the person but also other people. In our experience a tool that can ease traumatic stress responses is necessary for reconciliation. TTT has the advantage of being easy to spread to many on a grass root level.

Reconciliation after the genocide in Rwanda

For 100 days, from April to July in 1994, a genocide took place in Rwanda. It was well planned using media, fear and prejudice, similar to how the Nazis laid ground for the Holocaust in Europe. In Rwanda the target group was the people called Tutsis. To make way for the genocide this target group was dehumanized by the perpetrators. In Rwanda the Tutsis were called "cockroaches" and "snakes", "dangerous" and "unwanted animals". In spite of early warnings from the UN General in Rwanda, Romeo Dallaire, the international community did nothing to stop the massacre. More than 800000 people were killed.

Every person in the country was affected. Imagine being one of the thousands forced to kill, or being subjected to or witnessing the horrendous violence. The only way to build up a society after such experiences is to reconcile, but traumatic stress needs to heal for this to happen.

When people suffer from traumatic stress, aggression levels rise. This became very clear during TTT trainings in South Sudan where one of the participants shared his vision for the country five years ahead:

"I hope that by then if I happen to step on somebody's toe, I can say 'I am sorry' and he will be okay with that and no outburst of aggression will follow."

The term mass traumatization is relevant in places like Rwanda, South Sudan and Congo, but also in a lot of other countries including the USA, Israel, Palestine and the Balkans. To deal with this we need methods that can heal many at the same time. One such tool is the Trauma Tapping Technique.

What We do and Why

"Be the change you want to see in the world."

Mahatma Gandhi

Our organization, Peaceful Heart Network, is a non-profit organization with a small outfit of people. The main aim is to spread the Trauma Tapping Technique where possible. To do so we rely on donations, and getting paid for our workshops and seminars, creating a fund which can be used for going to places where our help is requested.

How do we handle it when somebody says *"I want to be a part of what you are doing"*?

We say *"Thank you, how do you wish to contribute?"*

When you work with us we will rely on you being engaged, congruent and ready to organize yourself and your contributions.

"What about money?"

We have no employees, we have limited funds and we strive to achieve big results with them. In order to do so we will, whenever possible:

- Cover the costs of local Trauma Tappers, like those in our centers in Mumosho and Bukavu in Congo and Rwanda.
- Pay for materials, transportation and water during trainings.

If you want to create a workshop, you can apply as a Peace Project on our website.

We get donations from people, companies and organizations who appreciate the need for our work and want to support it.

What kind of bricklayer are you?

One story that summarizes what it may mean to work non-profit, is the story of three bricklayers working to build a large church, mosque, community centre or something of this sort. As the story goes, three bricklayers were working side by side:

When asked, "What are you doing?" the first bricklayer replied:

"I'm laying bricks."

Then the second bricklayer was asked. He answered:

"I'm feeding my family."

The third bricklayer, when asked the same question, responded:

"I'm building a meeting place between man and God for times of sorrow, joy, christening, marriage and funeral."

Do You Want to Join?

You are welcome, providing you can organize yourself in every way. You must have your own insurance and be fully responsible for your own health. You will need to be used to traveling under simple conditions. You also must have informed yourself what it means to travel in these foreign areas and have the proper documents to do so.

We can help and support you in everything that has to do with spreading tools for healing trauma in the form of TTT and the related techniques we teach. We can train you and share our experiences. We can provide the materials. Welcome!

Trauma Tapping Centers

Amani Matabaro, who is the coordinator for our TTT center in Mumosho in eastern Congo, sent us this email:

"Mumosho is one of the war affected places in the eastern Congo which has remained with no humanitarian assistance. During the wars of invasion against Congo, Mumosho has served as a port of entry to foreign troops and prior to that the area has hosted a huge amount of the refugees after the 1994 Rwandan genocide, hence Mumosho has been affected on several dimensions.

Several attacks by armed groups have terrorized people in Mumosho. Not only these have been the problems but also SINELAC, a Great Lakes Region power company and Pharmakina, a German company known for their Quinine Malaria medicine project, have put all the fertile lands in Mumosho on a compulsory purchase request order.

All this together has left almost everyone in the community so poor, desperate, frustrated, living with everyday fear, traumatized, sad, angry, jumpy and anxious."

Amani Matabaro is a peace activist and model of reconciliation. He runs a local Non Government Organization (NGO) to support his home community Mumosho, located just on the border to Rwanda, a scene of atrocities during the years of conflict and war in the area.

Amani invited us to do a workshop with one of the women's organizations there. Thirty women came to the meeting. One of the participants said it would be good to have a special place, a center or a clinic, where people could come and get this kind of treatment. We agreed to make a pilot project with Amani to evaluate the results.

The same initiative came from our colleague Germando Bahathi, a trained nurse who has been working with rehabilitation of former child soldiers at

BVES rehabilitation center in Bukavu, and in that work experienced how TTT had helped many of them. Apart from his work at BVES he took on the responsibility for a TTT center in one of the communities of Bukavu, the capital of south Kivu.

In 2012 our organization, Peaceful Heart Network, formally decided to run these two Trauma Tapping centers with local counselors for an indefinite period of time.

Apart from receiving clients in the centers, the Trauma Tappers also do outreach to schools, churches and health centers, which now refer clients with certain symptoms to the TTT center.

Amani concludes the effect of the centers like this:

"Soon after the TTT center had opened in the area, most of the clients who have attended and taken TTT as a treatment have gradually been recovering from their symptoms, which for a very long time have affected their thoughts and emotions. Many of those who come to the center tell that they have recovered from insomnia, everyday headache, fatigue and many other symptoms of emotional stress.

There is need to disseminate the TTT treatment at a very large scale, make it sustainable at different community levels and this includes schools, health facilities and other places with large populations. TTT in Mumosho has shown it is an efficient treatment, and only requires an effective dissemination approach to reach those in need! It is necessary also with more trainings in schools for teachers to become able to handle war affected kids."

TTT – Peace Tapping Reports

This is the information visitors to our centers are asked for:

Month of treatment
Country
Peace Tapping Centre
Reporting Trauma Tapper
Beneficiary Name
Gender
Age
Traumatic life experience
Symptoms/Feelings

Symptom recurrence
- Are some of the symptoms there 24 hours a day, at night, in specific situations and/or only when thinking about it?
- Some symptoms most of the time?
- Some symptoms mostly at night?
- Some symptoms in specific situations?
- Some symptoms only when thinking about it?
- Other comments

SUD (1–10) before TTT
SUD (1–10) after TTT
Reflections after treatment
Symptoms that disappeared directly after the treatment

Follow-up
Follow-up of same person
Symptoms that disappeared some time after the treatment
Reflections some time after treatment
Symptoms or feelings remaining
Remaining symptom or feeling recurrence

Statistics

The Trauma Tapping Centers allow us to keep records of treatments and follow up the effects in an organized way.

When we revise the documentation of the cases treated in Bukavu, we have promising results. Over 85% of the treated experience improvements after a single session. The statistics for 620 cases over a period of 12 months is this:

Frequency (SUD (1–10) before TTT)

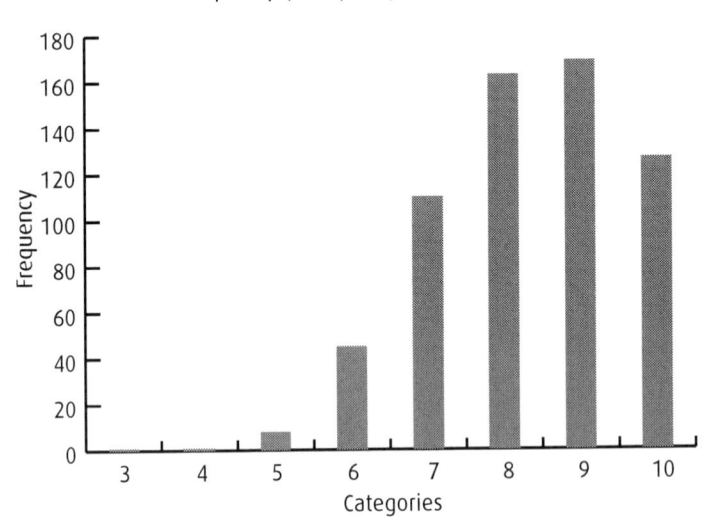

Frequency (SUD (1–10) after TTT)

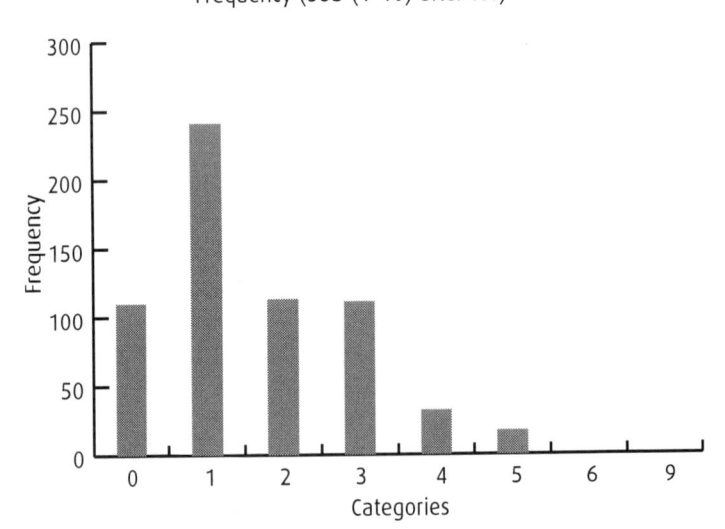

Resolving Yesterday - First Aid for Stress and Trauma with TTT

Certified Trauma Tapper

When we teach TTT we offer the possibility of becoming certified to our standards of what a Certified Trauma Tapper should know. Certification is no guarantee of the quality of a person's knowledge and skills, but it is a way for you to know what we think is important.

We only certify people who have been trained by somebody in our network. This means that we have a basic calibration of the person's social skills and emotional balance when interacting with others.

Since all skills are part theory and part practice the certification process has two steps:
1. Verify your theoretical knowledge by answering the assessment questions
2. Verify your practical experience by reporting the number of client sessions required

Once you are certified you will receive a certificate, and you will also be verified as a certified Trauma Tapper on our website.

Code of Ethics
To become a certified Trauma Tappers you have to vow to this code of ethics.

1. Beneficiary Welfare
   The welfare of your beneficiary is your primary concern at all times.

2. Trauma Tapping can be free
   As a certified Trauma Tapper you vow to treat people with needs even if they have no resources, within the realm of your situation.

3. Your Service
   You will always offer the service of Trauma Tapping as a complementary treatment, a first aid tool. Any other treatment the beneficiary is getting such as therapy or medication has nothing to do with this.

4. Your Skills and Certifications
   You acknowledge that some skills are acquired through certification and some only through dedication, devotion and continuous practice. It is therefore necessary that you:
   - Vow to take responsibility for your skills and certifications and make sure you are clear about this when asked.
   - Help and share your experiences and tools with other members.
   - Maintain an awareness of research and developments in the field of Trauma and other linked fields with an open mind.

5. War and abuse
   Remember when dealing with victims of war and abuse that every victim has a mindset you may want to understand and respect. A soldier is taught to be strong, an abused woman or child may back away from physical contact. Adapt your approach to every beneficiary and their unique situation. When you deal with beneficiaries under the age of 18 years or with special needs, it may be appropriate to do so with the informed consent of a parent or legal guardian if possible.

6. Trauma Tapping is free
   Encourage every person who is interested that they can learn Trauma Tapping. Inspire them to visit and download the free materials on our website www.peacefulheart.se and advocate that this is a first aid tool for everyone to learn and use.

7. Questions about TTT
   If you or anyone you meet has questions about TTT please contact us – we are here to serve, because your interest is ours.

Disclaimer: The Code does not assume that individual members possess particular levels of skill in any specific area; it is important, therefore, that users of members' services do satisfy themselves that the person they are working with is appropriately skilled. Peaceful Heart Network will deal with any infringements of the Code of Ethics through its Complaints and Disciplinary Procedure.

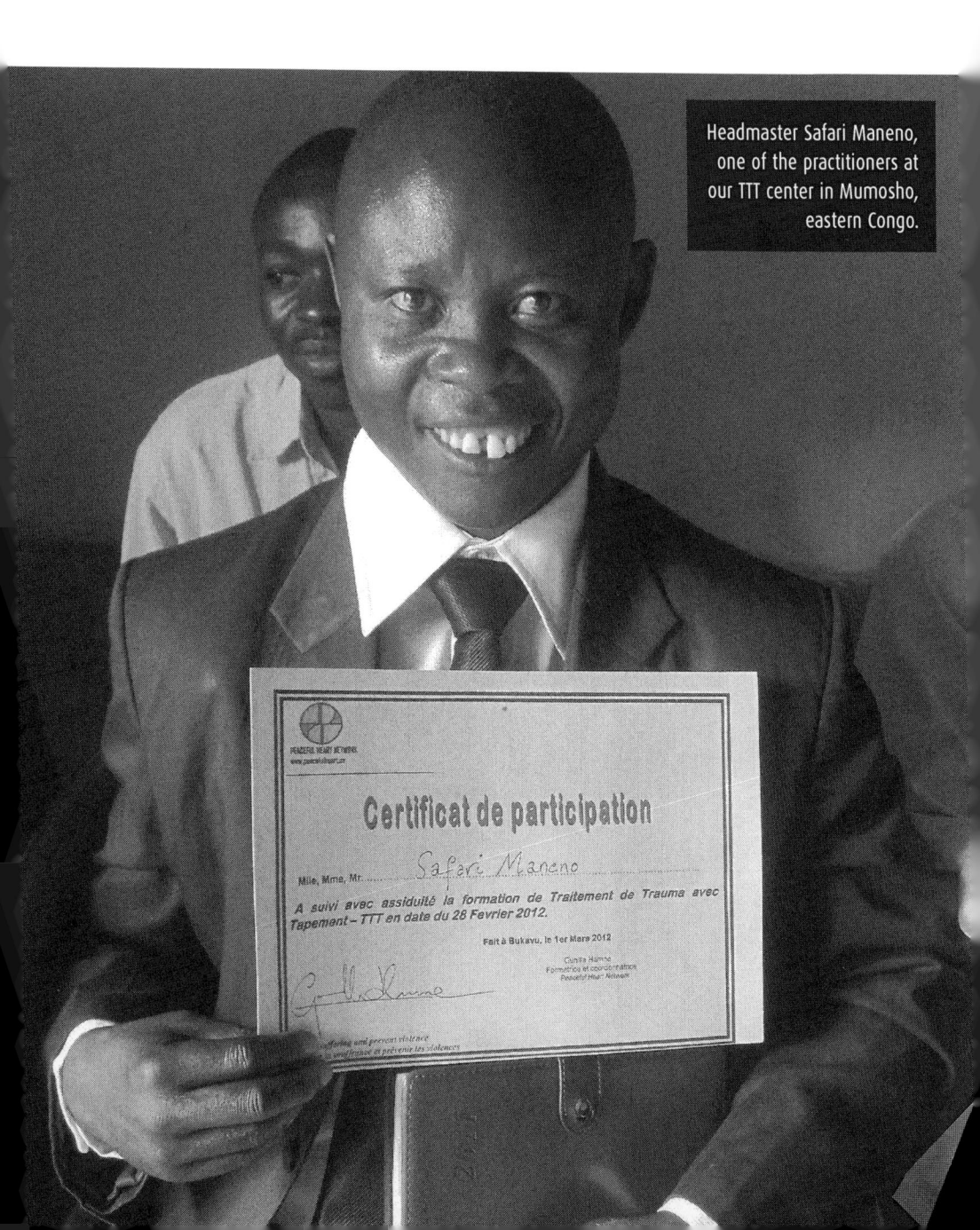

Headmaster Safari Maneno, one of the practitioners at our TTT center in Mumosho, eastern Congo.

Distributing TTT calendars at a Sevota reconciliation group in Rwanda.

Spreading the News

We constantly look for new ways of spreading information about how to handle emotional- and post-traumatic stress using TTT.

Filmed Materials

Some have learned TTT from watching the videos on our website, for example, and one of these is our colleague and hypnotherapist Fredrik Praesto in Sweden. He had a client who he didn't succeed in coaching because of language problems. Fredrik remembered hearing about TTT and looked up the website at his computer in the office while the client was waiting in the clinic. Here is his story:

"A couple of years back I helped Marie to get rid of her spider phobia using hypnosis and the Fast Phobia Cure. She was so impressed with the result that she sent her entire family and many of her friends to me for different issues.

About a year ago it was time for her mother, who suffered from a lot of stress and needed help to relax. Marie asked me if she could join to translate since her mother didn't speak Swedish or English. 'Sure', I said, 'That shouldn't present a problem.'

The session didn't go quite the way I had thought since it turned out that her mother had a severe hearing problem and was almost deaf. Marie had never realized this since as mother and daughter they understood each other pretty well. I was struggling to get some kind of result and time was running out with only twenty minutes until my next client was expected.

Suddenly an idea struck me. I remembered my friend Ulf had told me about this tapping technique that you could use without speaking the same language. I told Marie and her mother that I was going to check something on Youtube (maybe this didn't sound all too serious, but then again I knew Marie had great respect for my work).

So I checked the instruction video and took notes, turned back to Marie's mother and started the TTT session. To my surprise she suddenly looked calm and told me that her level of stress had gone down significantly.

Later I participated in a TTT-training and learned that the way I did it in that session was far from perfect, but still good enough. I think this is one of the beauties with this method. It's easy to learn and even if you don't do it perfectly you often get good results anyway. I've used TTT as part of my toolbox ever since."

Printed Materials

One challenge has been to print materials that can be reproduced locally at low cost, and that carry as little language content as possible to avoid translation issues.

A Calendar or a Poster

Printed materials are usually thrown away or lost. However, in many countries a calendar or poster will usually be allowed to stay on a wall in a home, school or church.

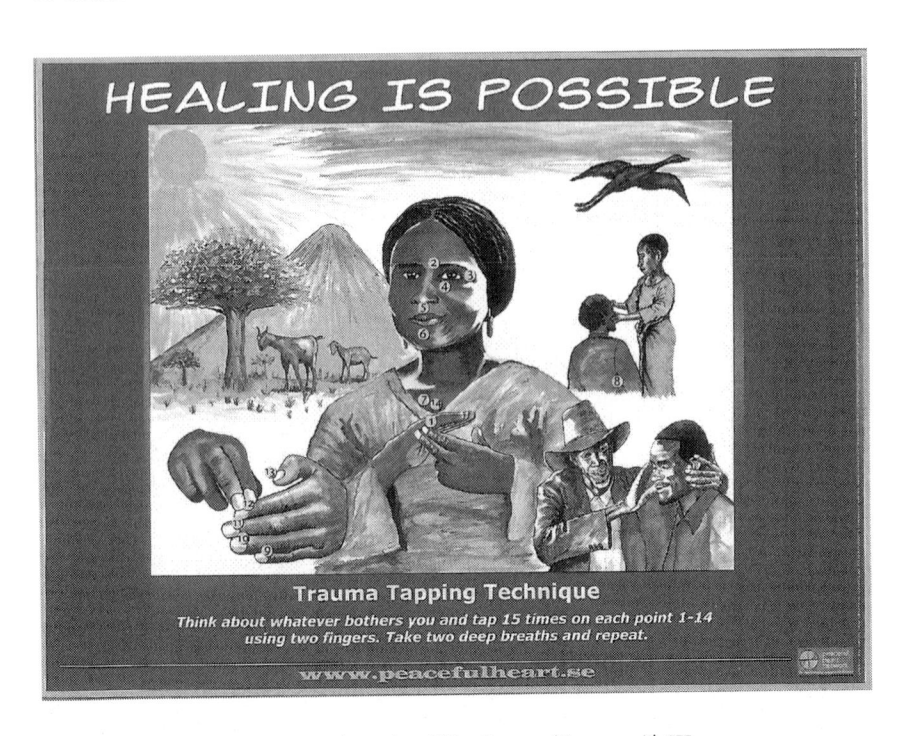

HEALING IS POSSIBLE

Trauma Tapping Technique
Think about whatever bothers you and tap 15 times on each point 1-14 using two fingers. Take two deep breaths and repeat.
www.peacefulheart.se

This is our first calendar and poster that we distributed several thousands of in Rwanda and Congo. The artist is Benard Githogori from Kenya. The idea was to bring hope through the woman's smile, the landscape with a sun of inspiration, a bird flying away that may be interpreted as a metaphor for sorrow leaving and men, women and children doing the tapping.

Instruction Manuals

There are also manuals and picture-based instructions for workshops and more in depth studies for free downloading on our website.

An illustration without words

We have created an illustration without words that explains the Trauma Tapping procedure.

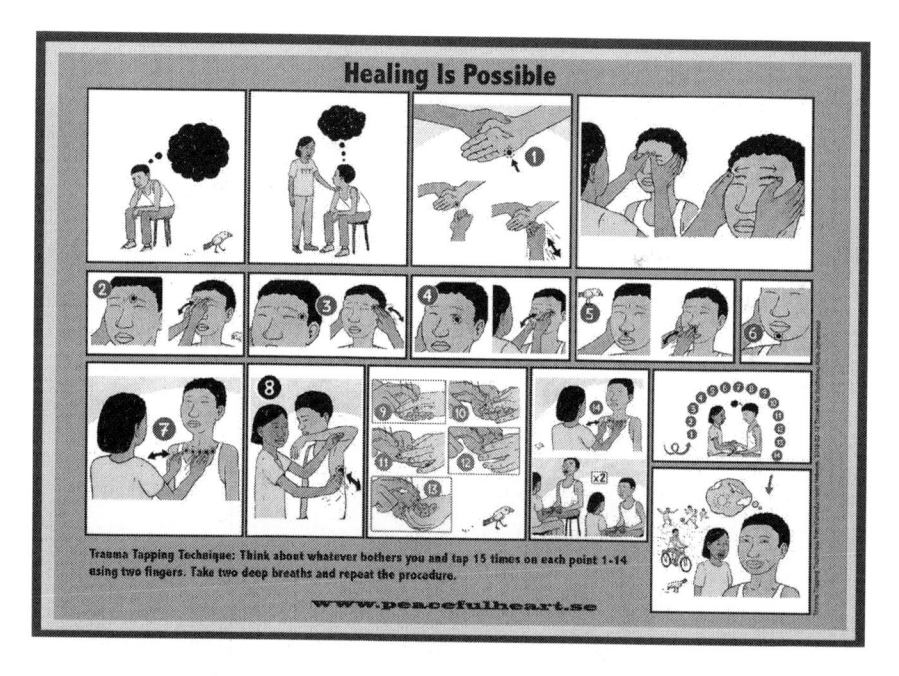

A Mobile Application

To spread the instruction for TTT digitally our web expert Nils Ola Nilsson has created a simple html-5 application that you can view and download in any computer, smartphone or mobile device. Check it out on our website: peacefulheart.se/app

The Multiplying Effect

"It is now over 7 000 refugees, who have been trained in TTT", said Murigo over the phone. *"There are 17 000 in the camp, how many can we reach?"*

Whole refugee families live in houses of plastic sheets, 4x3 meters in size, tightly packed together on the sloops of one hill in Rwanda. Forget privacy or what could be called a normal life. But still: it is safe. Not like the situation they left on the other side of the border.

Murigo met one of the members of the refugee committee, Chairman Benjamin, when he was in Kigali to arrange some documents. He told Murigo about his and the other refugees' experiences: being chased away from their homes in Congo, their belongings and cattle looted, houses burnt and people killed. Murigo said she had been through similar things during the genocide in Rwanda and added:

"Would you like to learn a technique that has helped me a lot?" asked Murigo.

Benjamin instantly replied *"Yes, please! We need that!"*.

Some days later she took the bus to the camp and trained eight members of the committee. A couple of weeks later when I (Gunilla) came back with her there were already 40 who knew the technique, since the first eight had done what Murigo had told them to do, they had trained five people each. Eight times five makes 40.

We met these 40 refugees in a local bar since we were not allowed to enter the camp itself without a special permit. Squeezing on benches all managed to get in. *"We are used to squeezing"*, the president joked. *"We live in plastic houses of 3x4 meters for a whole family."*

They were all very enthusiastic and eager to know more about TTT, and how to deal with internal images of violence and atrocities that many of them lived with. We demonstrated our videos from other trainings and did our best to answer their questions.

"Can we use TTT for children? Some scream from nightmares almost every night."

"Yes."

"Are those who just talk to themselves like a crazy person maybe traumatized?"

"Yes."

"Some don't eat, can that be a symptom of trauma?"

"Yes."

"How often can we use TTT?"

"As often as you want."

On their request we repeated the TTT. One after the other stood up and showed that they now could do it by themselves.

An Orange Bracelet

When there were more than 500 Trauma Tappers in the refugee camp, Murigo suggested that we should make it visible who they were, in some way.

"Why not some kind of bracelets?" she said.

The result is an orange silicone bracelet with the text:

Fingertips Heal Trauma – TTT – www.peacefulheart.se

The bracelet has become one more tool in the multiplying process of spreading trauma relief in the form of TTT.

To fully understand the extent of what Murigo is doing, and why this is significant in many ways, you might appreciate her personal story:

Murigo, a Generous Survivor

"During the genocide of 1994 in Rwanda I was hiding in the church in Kayonza together with a lot of people. The church was full, you could hardly move or find space to lay down and rest. We were there for two weeks, but then one morning the killer came – we heard them shouting and singing songs about how they were coming to get us. There were so many of them, what could we do?

They threw in burning mattresses and people panicked. They stormed the church with machetes and clubs, killing people around me. I recognized several of the killers, they were men and boys from our community, some were my neighbors others were local leaders of our area. They all came to kill us. They started swinging their machetes, and soon there was blood everywhere. Children, women and men were screaming.

I looked around, desperately searching for a way out. I was so small, only eight years old, and I ran as fast as I could and managed to squeeze myself out between the iron bars in one of the windows. I jumped to the ground and climbed a tree, my throat so tight that it felt like I was suffocating. From the tree I saw them kill people below me, but the killers didn't see me. How long did I sit there? I don't know. My fear made time stop.

After the genocide, me and my sister that survived came to live with the only aunt we had left – she was the sister of my mother and was married to my uncle. We used to live together as a big family before the genocide. Now it was only her and her two children, plus my sister and me left. Imagine!

Long after the genocide was over, we lived with fear that the Interhamwe would come and finish their job, to kill all Tutsis. Government soldiers had to escort us to school because the Interhamwe continued to attack even children like us. I suppose they did so because they had been told all Tutsis were bad. When they finally found and identified the bodies of my parents it became even more dangerous, because it became clear where they had been killed and by whom.

Even though three years had passed since the genocide it was unbearable. We could not live like this and the soldiers told my aunt to let me and my sister move to Kabuga to go to school there. Since the people we moved to were no relatives of mine, I offered to work in the house even though I was going to school, so that they wouldn't feel that it was a burden to take care of me."

I met Murigo during the first training that Dr. Johnson and I had with orphans of the genocide in 2007. When Murigo got certified as a Trauma Tapper she wrote this testimony for our website:

"Without TTT I don't know if I would be alive today. You know in 1994 I lost all my family. I did not feel good. I could not sleep in the night. I was crying a lot. I couldn't do anything to help myself. I couldn't think about future. I didn't like to go back to university. In fact I was feeling lonely all the time and my body was very weak.

The tapping treatment has changed many things in me. Now I can sleep. I have no more headaches. No more crying. I have gone back to university and my body is much stronger. I can laugh now. I will do TTT wherever I go!"

Today Murigo is in her late twenties and has finished studies in tourism at a university in Kigali. She has opened a restaurant big enough for wedding ceremonies in a highly populated area of the capital. She loves receiving the guests. You can tell from her smile.

Mukamurigo Veneranda, one of the most active TTT trainers in Rwanda.

Apart from managing her business she constantly takes initiatives to teach people TTT. She is dedicated because she feels that TTT saved her life. Now she shares this knowledge with people in similar situations.

Healing, and then what?

When we came to the women's group in Kiziguro we were met by frustration. Some weeks earlier we had conducted a session in the shade of the tall pine trees, where we had taught them how to handle traumatic stress and we had donated calendars to spread the TTT.

"*What is your frustration, do you not feel better after the treatment?*" we asked.

"*Yes, now we can see much more clearly thanks to the medicine (the Trauma Tapping) we got last time, and we realize that we have nowhere to go from here. We are poor, we live in small houses with mud floor and we do not have any cattle to sustain us, now what?*"

We never thought this far ahead and, to be honest it was quite a shock. Our aim has always been to spread a tool for emotional balance and survival to allow and empower people to move on in their lives. But what if there is nothing to move towards?

Cows, Goats or Chickens?

We thought about donating cows, but they are very sensitive animals that suddenly may require veterinary attention at a pretty high cost, which is out of the question for these women. Then we looked into donating goats, which are a pretty good bet in Africa. They eat anything and survive with a minimum of care. However it takes up to six months before they can start producing an income. We looked at a scheme of donating goats to groups of women and having them donate offspring to other groups, to create a multiplying effect. We started donating but soon realized that for this kind of help to work you need to be present on site. Follow them. Help them all the way. Chickens came up on the radar as well as pigs, but once we came this far we realized that this is not our infrastructure or mission, so we started looking for organizations already successfully involved in this area and integrating our Trauma Tapping with them and vice versa. We have realized that goats or chickens are not our way. We are instead, focusing on spreading First Aid for emotional and post-traumatic stress – TTT. Feel free to join us.

BVES, a rehabilitation center in Bukavu, Congo, for former child soldiers.

Lake Kivu, between Rwanda and Congo.

A WIDER PERSPECTIVE

Workshop with widows in Kamonyi, Rwanda

A Wider Perspective

Over the years Post Traumatic Stress Disorder (PTSD) has been considered a chronic syndrome that is hard to treat, especially after conflicts of war (Bou Khalil 2013). The two most common treatments are Cognitive Behavioral Therapy (CBT) and medication. In CBT there are positive results after a longer period of treatment, but at the same time there is a risk for re-traumatization due to the exposure nature of the therapy. With medication, symptoms are known to diminish temporarily, at the cost of other emotions also diminishing. At the same time the need to handle symptoms of post-traumatic stress is vital, due to how it affects personal health and suicidal inclination as well as being associated with a range of physical symptoms such as chronic musculoskeletal pain, hypertension, hyperlipidaemia, obesity and cardiovascular disease. (McFarlane 2010). In the long run it affects stability in families and society.

With over 3 million people in Rwanda suffering from symptoms of PTSD (Gishoma et al., 2014) we sense the need to take a step back and consider an intervention that can be administered with very little training in a challenged area or group, similar to any other first aid technique. The Trauma Tapping Technique is a development of the technique used by Dr Carl Johnson to treat PTSD in Kosovo 2001 (Johnson, Shala, Sejdijaj, Odell, & Dabishevci, 2001). It has been designed specifically for multiplication, and our intention is to bring more perspectives into the equation and debate around how PTSD can be handled.

Psychological first aid is considered an appropriate initial intervention, but it does not serve a therapeutic or preventive function (Litz, Gray et al. 2002). Also when first aid is mentioned in the case of psychological trauma it is mainly focused on principles of safety such as promoting a sense of safety, calming, self-efficacy, connectedness and hope (Wade, Howard et al. 2013). We propose a routine addition of a symptom reducing technique like TTT that can be administered peer-to-peer in areas and situations similar to that of Rwanda.

The fact that post-traumatic stress disorder (PTSD) is considered longstanding, even chronic is something we challenge (Hogberg, Pagani et al. 2008). In our experience the symptoms will persist when untreated, but they can be resolved with amygdala depotentiation as shown in research (Hong, Song et al. 2009), and this is what we believe is achieved through sensory exposure methods like TTT (Ronald A. Ruden 2005).

One may debate allowing peer to peer, or laymen, administer first aid for symptoms of post-traumatic stress. The main fear in this case would be if a person suffers and abreaction during treatment. In our experience TTT does not involve abreactions of the kind that would require more qualified administrators. Even if an abreaction would happen in the remote areas in question, a first aid method like TTT is probably the only available treatment for miles around.

We consider it neglectful to refrain from spreading a tool like TTT since symptoms of PTSD such as nightmares, intrusive thoughts, flashbacks and others which are typically experienced by individuals suffering from PTSD, can be transferred onto their immediate surroundings in the form of a secondary trauma. Beyond this, a family member's PTSD is potentially transferable to subsequent generations, interfering with the psychological development of children. (Klaric, Kvesic et al. 2013).

We have chosen to treat all members of a community in an area with traumatic events ex juvantibus, which means without diagnosis of PTSD. Since most of the people in the area have been directly involved in traumatic experiences, a large number of them are liable to develop symptoms, with significant psychosocial meaning, such as possible substance abuse and other negative health outcomes. (Warner, Warner et al. 2013).

TTT will have an effect and involves very little effort or time and no cost. We focus on being able to reach as many as possible, and a longer, more formal procedure of diagnosing their symptoms would be more demanding of personal, require more administration and take longer time. In some cases it would also possibly be re-traumatizing.

We suggest that more objective methods for diagnosing stress such as Heart Rate Variability could be standardized and added to the field since the relation to post-traumatic stress has been indicated by studies where veterans with combat-related PTSD displayed significantly depressed HRV as compared to subjects without PTSD (Tan, Dao et al. 2011).

Our findings show that a single session of the first aid Trauma Tapping Technique seems to significantly lower the subjective symptoms of post-traumatic stress. Our results and experiences from working since 2007 in the same challenged areas indicates that TTT is a valid approach for improving mental and emotional health on a first aid level in zones of post-conflict. We invite studies to be repeated with a refined structure and the implications for the general health in the participants to be followed up as well – either on a personal level or by monitoring police and hospital reports of general aggression and psychosocially related violence or suicide. On one hand, exposure to violence can lead to post-traumatic disorder symptoms, and on the other hand both violent behavior and aggression are some of the symptoms of post-traumatic stress. You might say that post-traumatic stress contains violence (Begic and Jokic-Begic 2002).

We suggest more studies to be made in collaboration with researchers of several sciences: social science, health care and psychosocial health care.

We hypothesize that incorporating the Trauma Tapping Technique into daily routines as a preventive measure for people exposed to traumatic events is a simple, cost-effective action that will improve the quality of life for those subjected to the treatment.

References

Begic, D. and N. Jokic-Begic (2002). "Violent behaviour and post-traumatic stress disorder." Current Opinion in Psychiatry 15(6): 623-626.

Bou Khalil, R. (2013). "Where all and nothing is about mental health: beyond posttraumatic stress disorder for displaced Syrians." Am J Psychiatry 170(12): 1396-1397.

Gishoma, Darius, Brackelaire, Jean-Luc, Munyandamutsa, Naasson, Mujawayezu, Jane, Mohand, Achour Ait, & Kayiteshonga, Yvonne. (2014). Supportive-Expressive Group Therapy for People Experiencing Collective Traumatic Crisis During the Genocide Commemoration Period in Rwanda: Impact and Implications (Vol. 2).

Hogberg, G., et al. (2008). "Treatment of post-traumatic stress disorder with eye movement desensitization and reprocessing: Outcome is stable in 35-month follow-up." Psychiatry Research 159(1-2): 101-108.

Hong, I., et al. (2009). "Extinction of cued fear memory involves a distinct form of depotentiation at cortical input synapses onto the lateral amygdala." Eur J Neurosci 30(11): 2089-2099.

Johnson, Carl, Shala, Mustafe, Sejdijaj, Xhevdet, Odell, Robert, & Dabishevci, Kadengjika. (2001). Thought Field Therapy—Soothing the bad moments of Kosovo. Journal of Clinical Psychology, 57(10), 1237-1240. doi: 10.1002/jclp.1090

Klaric, M., et al. (2013). "Secondary traumatisation and systemic traumatic stress." Psychiatr Danub 25 Suppl 1: 29-36.

Litz, B. T., et al. (2002). "Early intervention for trauma: Current status and future directions." Clinical Psychology-Science and Practice 9(2): 112-134.

McFarlane, A. C. (2010). "The long-term costs of traumatic stress: intertwined physical and psychological consequences." World Psychiatry 9(1): 3-10.

Ronald A. Ruden, M., PhD. (2005). "Why Tapping Works A Sense For Healing." (March 2005).

Tan, G., et al. (2011). "Heart rate variability (HRV) and posttraumatic stress disorder (PTSD): a pilot study." Appl Psychophysiol Biofeedback 36(1): 27-35.

Wade, D., et al. (2013). "Early response to psychological trauma What GPs can do." Australian Family Physician 42(9): 610-614. Warner, C. H., et al. (2013). "Identifying and managing posttraumatic stress disorder." Am Fam Physician 88(12): 827-834.

Disclaimer

The authors of this book does not dispense medical advice or prescribe the use of any technique as a form of treatment for physical, emotional, or medical problems without the advice of a physician, either directly or indirectly. The intent of the authors is only to offer information of a general nature to help you in your quest for emotional well-being. In the event you use any of the information in this book for yourself or others, the authors assume no responsibility for your actions.

Glossary

9-gamut
9-gamut (nine-gamut) is a sequence of eye movements and verbal exercises for activating and balancing both hemispheres of the brain. Used in TFT, and as a separate method which we use at times, but not as part of the basic TTT protocol.

Abreaction
An abreaction, or flooding, is when somebody relives a traumatic experience as if it is happening again; a type of catharsis. There are therapies designed to heal by bringing abreactions about, with success, however, we have never yet seen the need for abreactions or flooding for healing of trauma in a session of TTT, and consider them both unnecessary and inhuman.

Alpha waves (see Brain wave patterns)

Adrenaline
Adrenaline is a hormone we produce during high stress or exciting situations, including when we experience a fight or flight response. Adrenaline stimulates the heart rate, contracts blood vessels, and dilates air passages, all of which will increase blood flow to our muscles and oxygen to our lungs. Long or intensive experiences of *fight or flight* situations that raise adrenaline levels will make us mentally and physically agitated until the hormone is out of our system. TTT, Do-In, constructive physical labor and the Blow-Out technique can help this leveling out, allowing us to relax.

Allergy
An allergy is a hypersensitive reaction of the immune system. Symptoms of an allergic reaction include red eyes, itchiness, swelling, runny nose, eczema, hives or an asthma attack. A session with TTT will at times release or diminish allergic symptoms. It remains open for more research to find if this is because the nervous system is calmed, or if maybe some allergic reactions are conditioned in the same way as symptoms of traumatic stress.

Alpha Theta Breathing
By consciously focusing on inhaling deeply using the diaphragm, and lengthening the time you hold the breath, and exhale in proportion to the time you breathe in will allow you to reach the slower alpha and theta brain wave levels, which are ideal for relaxation, guided imagery and hypnosis. We use the Alpha-Theta breathing twice between each round of Trauma Tapping in a complete TTT session.

AMPA Receptors
AMPA receptors are synapses in the amygdala that participate in fear learning, and are potentiated when a traumatic experience is encoded in the amygdala. They will stay encoded triggering the same fear reactions even after the event is over, unless depotentiated with a technique like TTT.

Amygdala
The amygdala is a set of neurons located deep in the brain, shown to play a key role in the processing of emotions. The amygdala is part of the limbic system. In humans and other animals, this subcortical brain structure is linked to both fear responses and pleasure. Conditions such as anxiety, autism, depression, post-traumatic stress disorder and phobias are suspected of being linked to the functioning of the amygdala. The main thesis of Dr. Ronald Ruden about sensory exposure treatments is that the amygdala is depotentiated, and the link between sensory memories from a traumatic event to the emotional and somatic responses is dissolved.

Amygdala Hijacking
We have a mind that thinks and a mind that feels. The research by Joseph Le Doux reported by Goleman (1995), states *"...the architecture of the brain gives the amygdala a privileged position as the emotional sentinel, able to hijack the brain."* This survival mechanism allows us to react to things before the rational brain has time to reflect. The amygdala in animals has been found able to respond in as little as twelve thousands of a second. The "radar" in the amygdala will constantly scan our environment for anything that may hurt us, and react in an instant. A post-traumatic stress reaction is an amygdala hijacking, reacting to stimuli similar to the encoding experience, by triggering AMPA receptors created at the time.

Anxiety
Anxiety is a feeling of fear, worry and uneasiness often accompanied by muscular tension, restlessness, fatigue and problems in concentration. Anxiety is a common symptom of emotional or post-traumatic stress that often is successfully alleviated with TTT.

Autonomic Nervous System
The autonomic nervous system (ANS) is a control system that functions regardless of consciousness (autonomically) to control life support functions such as heart rate, digestion, breathing, salivation, perspiration, pupillary dilation, urination, sexual arousal and swallowing. The control is shared with the somatic nervous system, which gives us voluntary control. The two major subdivisions of the ANS are the Sympathetic Nervous System (SNS) or "fight-or-flight" and the Parasympathetic Nervous System (PNS) or "rest and digest" subdivision, both of which act in concert with each other at all times. We find that the Autonomic Nervous System often will rebalance itself after a session of TTT.

Beta Waves (see Brain wave patterns)

Blow Out
A simple exercise for releasing pent up adrenaline, cortisol and carbon dioxide after a situation of tension, fear or aggression (fight or flight response).

Brain Wave Patterns
There are four major types of brainwave patterns that can be measured by electroencephalography (EEG). Rated from higher activity to lower they are Beta-, Alpha-, Theta- and Delta-waves. The Beta-wave activity is seen in normal waking consciousness, including busy or anxious thinking. These patterns are thought to represent the activity of the visual cortex in an idle state. Alpha waves are associated with relaxation when the eyes are opened or closed but still awake. Theta waves are associated with profound daydreams, lucid dreaming, light sleep and hypnosis. Delta waves appear in deep sleep and are believed to be part in depotentiation of the amygdala with psychosensory exposure (therapies) treatments such as TTT or Havening.

CBT – Cognitive Behavioral Therapy
Cognitive behavioral therapy (CBT) is a psychotherapeutic approach based on a number of goal-oriented, explicit systematic procedures built on exposure to the trigger stimuli. We find TTT a great add-on for this type of therapy, since it will depotentiate any responses that are triggered.

Child Soldier
In over twenty countries around the world, children are directly involved in war. Denied a childhood and often subjected to horrific violence, an estimated 200 000 to 300 000 children are serving as soldiers for both rebel groups and government forces in current armed conflicts. (Source: Human Rights Watch 2007)

Clean Language
A method for eliciting a client's metaphors and inducing positive change, developed by David Grove during over 30 years consisting of a small number of specifically worded questions.

Cognitive Psychology
Cognitive psychology is the study of mental processes such as attention span, the use of language, memory, perception, problem solving, creativity and reflective thinking.

Confidence
Confidence is a state of being certain about something, for example that a hypothesis or prediction is correct or that a specific course of action is the best or most effective compared to others.

Congruency
The word congruency comes from the Latin of "being together" or "in alignment with". In our context we mean that a person is congruent when thoughts, behaviors and feelings are in alignment with the person's core beliefs.

Content Free
Working therapeutically with a state or emotion, without trying to find a specific trigger event or root cause, is also called working "content free".

Cortisol
Cortisol is a hormone released in response to stress, to free available glucose for the brain by generating energy from stored reserves. Lower priority activities, such as the immune system, are diverted in order to react to, and survive, immediate threats. Prolonged cortisol secretion due to stress, may result in unwanted physiological changes.

Crown Pull
The Crown Pull is when you put your fingers in the middle of the forehead of a person (or yourself) and pull outwards to the sides of the head. The effect is calming. It is sometimes used as part of the TTT sequence.

Delta Waves (see Brain Wave Patterns)

Depotentiation
Traumatic stress is thought to be permanented by fear conditioning in the form of induced potentiation of surface AMPA receptors (AMPAR) at excitatory synapses in the lateral amygdala. These receptors act as a conditioned alarm for any of the stimuli present at the moment of potentiation (the traumatic event). Depotentiation, reversal of conditioning-induced potentiation, has been proposed as a cellular mechanism for fear extinction. This is the theory proposed to explain how TTT works.

Do-In
A Japanese self-massage exercise which energizes the body, calms down the nervous system and helps building resilience to trauma.

Dopamine
Dopamine is a neurotransmitter that is a vital part of the brain's reward- and pleasure centers and cognitive alertness. Dopamine also helps regulate movement and emotional responses. Dopamine enables us not only to become aware of possible rewards, but also to take action to move toward them (motivation).People with low dopamine activity may be more prone to addiction.

EFT- Emotional Freedom Technique
EFT is probably the most well-known version of the tapping methods. It was created by Gary Craig in late 1990`s as a simplified version of TFT.

EMDR - Eye Movement Desensitization and Reprocessing
Eye movement desensitization and reprocessing (EMDR) is a sensory exposure therapy developed by Francine Shapiro using eye movements as main sensory input. EMDR is usually done in a protocol that includes having the clients recalling distressing images while receiving one of several types of bilateral sensory input, including side to side eye movements. The use of EMDR was originally developed to treat adults suffering from PTSD. However, it is also used to treat other conditions and children.

Emotion
An emotion is a statement of our mind, or soul, about something. It is different from a feeling, which is noting something through our senses - for example feeling tired, hungry, happy, pressure or heat. There are theories stating five emotions similar to all cultures: love, hate, joy, sorrow, and fear. Research shows that emotions are involved in culture, social functioning, temperament, personality, health and biological variables such as physical diseases. Feelings are short indicators whereas emotions are moods that can last a long time. Emotional stress (hate, sorrow, fear) is an example.

Empowerment
In essence, empowerment is about having or taking more control over all aspects of your life. We regard the Trauma Tapping Technique as a tool for empowerment, because it allows anybody, even a child without formal schooling, to take control over their emotions, and to be able to help others do the same. To move from being a victim of violence in need of help from experts, to being a survivor that can help others heal, move on and survive is truly empowering.

Energy Psychology
Energy psychology is a term used to include EFT, TFT and other methods that base their explanation of their functionality on the perceived relationship between the energy system

of the body and mind as described in traditional Chinese medicine. The energy system is usually referred to as the body meridians.

Epinephrine (see Adrenaline)

Feeling
A feeling is a response to sensory input that can be real or imagined. Feelings can include both physical sensations as well as mental states. For example you can be feeling tired, hyper, jumpy and hungry. Most of feelings will pass when treated with rest, safety and/or medication.

Fight or Flight Response
The *fight or flight* response is an automatic biological reaction to acute stress that activates a number lifesaving and defense-optimizing mechanisms in our body-mind system. Adrenaline (epinephrine), norepinephrine and cortisol are released into our bloodstream creating an increase in circulation and energy to certain body systems, and a downshift of for that moment less important ones, such as immune system and digestion, into maintenance mode. In this way, the fight or flight response prepares us for extreme action.

First Aid
A first aid technique generally consists of simple, and in some cases potentially life-saving techniques that an individual can be trained to perform with minimal equipment. We regard TTT as a first aid technique for symptoms of emotional- and post-traumatic stress.

Flashback
A flashback is a sudden, usually powerful, re-experiencing of a past experience. It is a common symptom of post-traumatic stress.

Flooding (see Abreaction)

Frontal Cortex
The frontal cortex is the part of our brain where the logical, reflective and strategic thinking is located. When we are in extreme stress, such as when *fight or flight* response is activated, this part may shut off, which sometimes is called an "amygdala hijacking". TTT will help turn it back on.

Genocide
Genocide is a term for a systematic and deliberate destruction of an ethnic, religious or national group.

Glutamate
Glutamate is the primary excitatory (action creating) neurotransmitter at synapses in the central nervous system. It is a molecule that binds postsynaptic receptors such as the AMPA receptors of the amygdala, which will connect traumatic stimuli to emotional responses, and which we believe are depotentiated (unbound) in the process of applying TTT.

Gorilla Tapping
What we call gorilla tapping is tapping done under the collarbones – all over the upper part of the chest. It is efficient for dissolving anxiety, and is part of the TTT sequence. It can be used on its own for releasing stress. It is also similar to what gorillas do, which is why we call it Gorilla Tapping.

Havening
Havening is a psychosensory exposure therapy for emotional and post-traumatic stress developed by Dr. Ronald Ruden. It is in many ways similar to TTT, and we believe the science presented by Dr. Ruden applies to both methods.

Hypnotherapy
Hypnotherapy is a form of therapy with the aim of creating new responses, thoughts, attitudes, behaviors or feelings that is undertaken with a subject in hypnosis: a state of mind with heightened suggestibility and access to the subconscious mind. There are many different schools and traditions within clinical and experimental hypnosis. We find TTT an incredibly valuable addition to the toolbox of hypnotherapy.

IDP – Internally Displaced Person
Internally displaced persons are people who have been forced to flee their homes in order to avoid the effects of armed conflict, situations of generalized violence, violations of human rights, natural or human-made disasters, and who have not yet crossed an internationally recognized state border, in effect being refugees in their own country.

Karate Point
The first point used for tapping in the TTT sequence, located on the side of the hand opposite the thumb (from the little finger to the wrist.) Also known as Karate Chop.

Limbic System
The limbic system is a part of the brain sometimes called the mammalian or emotional brain and the home of the amygdala (see amygdala).

Meditation
The word meditation has different meanings in different situations. Meditation has been practiced for thousands of years as a component of many religious traditions. Meditation usually involves an effort to self-regulate the mind. Meditation is also used to clear the mind and health issues, such as high blood pressure, depression, and anxiety. There is a meditative element to TTT and many people go into a trance during a session.

Meridians
According to traditional Chinese medicine there is a web of energy channels in the body, called the meridians. Fourteen main meridians have been described, connected to, and named after their relation to inner organs. On the meridians there are specific treatment points used for acupuncture, acupressure, shiatsu and other body based treatments for somatic issues. There are almost 400 acupuncture points.

According to Chinese medicine, if the energy- (qi) flow of a person is disturbed the person can experience physical or emotional disease. When the flow is corrected the person will start healing. From this theory exercises such as Tai Chi, yoga and qigong have emanated. Although acupuncture is proven to work for a number of issues and is used in many medical treatments, it has not yet been possible to verify the existence of the meridians scientifically. The points of TTT are placed along these meridians.

Metaphor
A metaphor is a figurative comparison between one situation or object and another with the intent of conveying an understanding of the mechanisms involved. Most of our learning is metaphorical. Clean Language is an example of a therapeutic method focused on helping us define our metaphors and change them, in order to change our relation to life. Many of the testimonials after TTT sessions are metaphorical: *"A blanket was lifted"*, *"A weight fell of my shoulders"*, *"The noises in my head came to an end"*, *"Everything became brighter around me"*.

Mindfulness
Mindfulness is a stress reduction program created by Jon Kabat-Zinn, at the University of Massachusetts Medical School. It is based on a combination of meditation, western psychology and science. Mindfulness has shown to be useful to help people cope with stress, anxiety, pain and illness. We find TTT helps people become mindful.

Multiplier Effect
In economics, a multiplier is a factor of proportionality that measures how much a start variable can affect an outcome variable. The multiplier effect we refer to in this book is that of

teaching TTT as a first aid method to a number (x) of people that each teach it to a number (y) of people, causing the ripples of healing to multiply with x times y and so forth.

Neurons
A neuron is an electrically excitable cell (also called a nerve cell) that processes and transmits information through electrical and chemical signals. Neurons are the core components of the nervous system and an important part in the encoding and decoding of traumatic stress.

Neurotransmitters
Neurotransmitters are the chemicals that communicate information throughout our brain and body. They relay signals between nerve cells, called neurons. For example, the brain uses neurotransmitters to tell our heart to beat, our lungs to breathe, our stomach to digest. They also affect mood, sleep, concentration, weight, and can cause diverse symptoms when they are out of balance. We find that rebalancing the nervous system with TTT will affect breathing, mood, sleep and concentration positively. This suggests a balance is also created on a neurotransmitter level.

Nightmare
A nightmare is a dream that evokes an unpleasant or unwanted response. This is a common symptom of post-traumatic stress. Many people say that their nightmares stop after experiencing TTT.

NLP – Neuro Linguistic Programming
Neuro-linguistic programming (NLP) is an approach to communication, personal development and change created by Richard Bandler and John Grinder in the 1970s. The technique is based on the belief that there is a connection between our neurological processes ("neuro"), our use of language ("linguistics") and our behavioral patterns ("programming").

Nocebo
Nocebo is the negative healing effect of a negative belief.

Norepinephrine
Norepinephrine (also called noradrenaline) is both a hormone and neurotransmitter, regulated by the sympathetic nervous system to stop bleeding, increase heart rate, blood pressure and the sugar level of the blood. It is part of our *fight or flight* response. When experiencing symptoms of post-traumatic stress, norepinephrine levels rise.

Oxytocin
Oxytocin is a hormone typically known for the effect it has in facilitating childbirth, milk secretion, trust and attachment between individuals. However, oxytocin has a complex role, and is involved also in the perceptions of fear and anxiety. There is research showing that human touch will help produce oxytocin. We believe it may be a side-effect of TTT, but more research is needed.

Palpitation
Palpitation of the heart is an abnormal heartbeat that ranges from skipped beats to accelerated heart rate with dizziness or difficulty breathing as possible consequences. Palpitations may be brought on by post-traumatic stress, anxiety, panic, adrenaline, alcohol, nicotine, caffeine, cocaine, amphetamines and other drugs, disease or as a symptom of panic disorder. During palpitations TTT can be very effective.

Parasympathetic Nervous System
The parasympathetic nervous system (PNS) is a chief subdivision of the autonomic nervous system (ANS), and dominates functions of "rest and digest" when conditions do not require immediate action. The PNS promotes a slower heartbeat, a slower respiratory rate, increased perspiration and salivation, smaller pupils, enhanced waste disposal and sexual arousal. Most of the actions of the PNS are automatic. Some, such as breathing, work in concert with the conscious mind.

Pathfinder Cards
The Pathfinder Cards are a set of visual coaching cards inspired by NLP that we developed together with artist Osenele Ukpan to elicit internal solutions for a challenge by metaphorical association, regardless of language or learning skills.

Peer-to-Peer
A peer-to-peer network in computer terms, is a network architecture in which individual nodes in the network (called peers) act as both suppliers and consumers of resources, in contrast to a centralized client–server model, where client nodes request access to resources provided by central servers. In this context we refer to our ways of teaching TTT as a peer-to-peer model of distribution.

Phobia
A phobia is an overwhelming fear of a stimulus that may not be dangerous at all. Often a session of TTT will resolve a phobia, especially if applied when the phobic fear is activated.

Placebo
Placebo is the positive healing effect of a positive belief.

Possession by Demons
Demonic possession is supposed by many belief systems to be the spirit possession of an individual, by a malevolent being, referred to as a demon. Sometimes in some areas a person with symptoms of emotional and post-traumatic stress will behave in a way that is perceived as or explained as being possessed by a demon. Providing a session of TTT can save their lives, literally, since possession by demons often is feared and treated with aggression.

Post Traumatic Growth
Positive psychological change experienced as a result of the struggle with highly challenging life circumstances. Very often disconnecting the emotional reactions from traumatic memories with a depotentiation method like TTT, will allow for this to take place, making people stronger than before the experiences.

Post-Traumatic Stress
A stress reaction that triggers or persists after the traumatic encoding event has passed, as if the event is still happening. TTT is about alleviating this.

Psychosensory
Psychosensory describes our mental perception and interpretation of sensory stimuli. TTT is part of a field of psychosensory exposure treatments.

PTSD
PTSD or Post-Traumatic Stress Disorder is a diagnosis used for describing a number of symptoms that may occur in a person who has lived through one or several highly stressful (traumatic) events such as accidents, sexual assault, loss of loved ones or war. The symptoms are many and include flashbacks, hyper arousal, emotional numbness, depression and anxiety. We think of it as an alarm that needs to be reset, rather than a disorder, and therefore refer to it as post-traumatic stress.

Re-traumatization
Re-traumatization, is when the negative impact of an event is reinforced. This is one of the reasons TTT- trainers don't go into verbal details of a client's experiences, it is never needed.

Resilience
Resilience is our ability to adapt and rebuild our lives after being exposed to situations of extreme stress and tragedy. It is something many believe we can train, and that is devel-

oped in the eye of adversity. It is found in a combination of behaviors, thoughts and actions that can be learned.

Scientific Method
A scientific method is a technique used to investigate something unknown in nature and gain new knowledge. It is based on empirical and measurable evidence.

Scientific Theory
A scientific theory is an explanation of something in nature and acquired through a scientific method. It also has to be confirmed in a repeated manner through experiments and/or observations.

Secondary Trauma
Secondary trauma is a form of post-traumatic stress resulting from exposure to traumatized or suffering persons through work or acquaintance. Anybody working with, or under influence/presence of traumatized persons should always be aware of this risk and treat themselves and their colleagues preventively, with TTT or otherwise.

Self-Medication
Self-medication is when an individual uses a substance or behavior to self-administer treatment for an often unmanaged, undiagnosed physical or psychological ailment – for example drinking to escape anxiety or gambling to raise low dopamine levels. We recommend TTT when the urge, or feelings about having the urge, are present.

Senses
Living creatures perceive the world through their senses, such as sight, hearing, smell, taste, touch and balance/movement. All memories are coded through the senses. We store our memories through a perception of a sense. This can be for example a perception of a smell or a sight and the person is instantly reminded of a situation in the past. Each experience of the senses can act as a trigger and occurs for pleasant as for unpleasant memories alike. So, if a traumatic experience is encoded, all details of the traumatic moment will be part of the memory, thus making it possible that a sensed detail will trigger the traumatic experience again. Depotentiating techniques like TTT will disconnect the emotional responses, allowing a person to have the perception of the details without triggering the stress response.

Sensory
A sensory system consists of sensory receptors, which are neural pathways in our nervous system and parts of the brain involved in sensory perception. (see Senses)

Sensory Exposure Therapy
A Sensory Exposure Therapy relies on a) being exposed to an emotional reaction to a stimuli b) an intervention through one or more of our sensory systems. (See Sensory).

Serotonin
Serotonin is a neurotransmitter, a type of chemical that helps relay signals from one area of the brain to another. Most brain cells are influenced either directly or indirectly by serotonin. This includes brain cells related to mood, sexual desire and function, appetite, sleep, memory and learning, temperature regulation and some social behavior. In terms of our body function, serotonin can also affect the functioning of our cardiovascular system (heart/blood), muscles, and various elements of the endocrine (hormonal) system. Although it is widely believed that a serotonin deficiency plays a role in depression, there is no way to measure its levels in the living brain.

Sex slave
Sexual slavery is a crime in the form of enslavement which includes forced sexual activity. In contrast to the crime of rape, which is a completed offence, sexual slavery constitutes a continuing offence. Both sexual slavery and rape are traumatic experiences that can lead to symptoms of stress, even many years later, often triggered by a second, sometimes unrelated, traumatic experience.

Somatic
The word somatic comes from Greek and means "of the body", i.e. relating to the body – distinct from the mind, soul, or spirit. In medicine, somatic illness is bodily, not mental, illness. When a disease of the body comes from an imbalance of the mind, it is called psychiatric or psychosomatic. TTT is applied on the resulting unwanted sensation or emotion, reaching both body and mind.

Somatic Poem
In this context we refer to a poem we use as a setup before a group training of TTT, to make sure everybody connects with the bodily senses (smell, hearing, touch, taste and vision) related to memories of emotional or traumatic stress.

Stress
Stress is a description of a response to something that is perceived as a threat to our well-being. A stress response can have physical, mental and/or emotional effects. In small doses stress is part of our normal feedback mechanisms in life. Having too much stress over a longer time can cause medical problems such as anxiety, irritable bowel syndrome (IBS),

tense shoulders, aggression and post-traumatic stress. These symptoms will often disappear over time as a result of a session with TTT.

Sub Cortex
The sub cortex is the part of the brain involved in motor control and skill learning. It has three main divisions: the limbic system, the thalamus and the hypothalamus. The limbic system is involved in the detection and expression of emotion, including the amygdala for the *fight or flight* response and the hippocampus for learning, laughter and positive feelings. The thalamus is the main sensory relay for all senses except smell and the hypothalamus is responsible for body temperature, hunger, sexual behavior and thirst.

SUD – Subjective Units of Distress
SUD is a subjective scale for measuring/calibrating an emotional response that is done by the person being treated. The scale is from 0–10, where 0 is no discomfort, and 10 is maximum discomfort. This is done before and after individual sessions, to provide feedback both for the person treating and the person being treated.

Summary Trauma
Summary trauma is a term we use when symptoms of post-traumatic stress have developed over a longer time, and not necessarily by events that are linked. The symptoms are a summary of traumatic experiences, but the mechanisms and the possibility to resolve them with TTT are the same.

Survival
To survive is to remain alive. All living creatures have a built-in systems and strategies for survival. Sometimes survival mechanisms are "jammed", resulting in constant vigilance. The usefulness of TTT is to reset this mechanism so survival can continue on a normal level.

Sympathetic Nervous System
The sympathetic nervous system (SNS) is part of the autonomic nervous system (ANS), and controls involuntary body functions such as digestion, breathing etc. Its general action is to mobilize the body's *fight or flight* response. It is, however, constantly active at a basic level to maintain homeostasis. Post-traumatic stress is a sign that this system is over-activated. TTT help us reset it back to normal.

Symptom
A symptom can be defined as any emotion, imbalance, or disease which is noticed by the patient and thought of as an expression or sign of something that has caused it. A symptom differs from the normal functions or perceptions of a person.

For example, sneezing can be a symptom of having a cold, an allergic reaction, or having inhaled sneezing powder. In our context we speak of symptoms of emotional or post-traumatic stress which include a number of symptoms: Self-medication, flashbacks, nightmares, anxiety, loss of hope, tunnel vision etc. Most of these symptoms can be relieved with one or more sessions of TTT.

Synapse
In the nervous system, a neuron passes its chemical and electrical signals through a structure called a synapse. The synapse is the means to create a connection from one cell to another. The AMPA receptors (see AMPA receptors) are synapses in the amygdala.

Taoism
Taoism is a philosophical, ethical and religious tradition of Chinese origin. In this context Taoism denotes something that is both the source and the driving force behind everything that exists. We find a lot of useful sayings and stories in the tradition of Taoism that we sometimes quote at workshops of TTT.

TAT – Tapas Acupressure Technique
TAT is a method for treating symptoms of trauma by holding one hand on the back of the head and the other hand on the forehead (alternatively placing three fingers on specific acupuncture points around the upper part of the nose).

TFT – Thought Field Therapy
TFT was the first method using tapping for healing symptoms of emotional stress. It was created by Dr. Roger Callahan in the early 1980's. TTT can be described to relate to TFT as a non-verbal first aid version that rests on a different set of presuppositions about the mechanisms involved.

Psychological Trauma
Psychological trauma is a conditioning reflex in our mind that is formed as the result of a severely distressing event with an importance to us, from which we perceived that there was no escape from, or solution to, at the time.

TTT – Trauma Tapping Technique
A first aid sensory exposure technique for alleviating symptoms of emotional- and post-traumatic stress that is optimized for spreading through multiplication.

TTT Song
TTT can be taught and applied in the form of a song, which is very effective with large groups.

Tunnel vision
The loss of peripheral vision resulting in a tunnel-like field of vision, often due to a stress reaction in the Autonomic Nervous System. Tunnel vision is a symptom that may disappear after a session of TTT.

Vicarious Trauma (See Secondary Trauma)

Index

Aggression 128
Alarm Mode 119
Allergies 122
Alpha-Theta Breathing 164
Anger 133
Anxiety 128, 133
Balancing the Brain 165
Behaviors 128
Blow-Out 168
Breathing 121
Carl Johnson 35
Certified Trauma Tapper 187
Children 69
Child soldiers 137
Church 111
Clean Language 157
Compassion 149
Congruency 52
Cortisol 120
Crown Pull 161
Decoding 123
Depotentiation 125
Difficulty breathing 133
Difficulty trusting 133
Dissociation from body 133
Do-in Self Massage 166
EMDR 156
Emotions 127
Empathizing 149
Empowerment 109
Encoding 123
Evolution of TTT 35
Exercise 153
Fear 133
Feeling Empty 62
Feeling isolated 133
Feeling weak 133
Feeling worthless 133
Fight, Flight, Freeze or Faint 120
First Aid 31
Flashbacks 128
Forgetfulness 133
Gary Craig 35
Gorilla Tapping 162
Groups 93
Guilt 128
Gunilla Hamne 7
Havening 156
Headache 61
Head Holding 163
Hypertension 133
Hypnotherapy 157
IEMT 156
Instability 133
Irritation 133
Limiting mindsets 147
Medication 155
Meditate 153
Meridians 125
Metaphors of Healing 84
Military Experience of TTT 79
Mindfulness 156
Mindset for Survival 145
Mobile Application 193
Multiplication 110
Multiplying Effect 194
Nausea 61
Nightmares 128
NLP 157
Nocebo 56
Orange Bracelet 195
Palpitation 133
Parasympathetic nervous system 119
Pathfinder Cards 170
Persisting Symptoms 132
Phobias 122
Placebo 56
Positive Intentions 128
Positive Tapping 151
Possession by Demons 142
Poster 192
Post Traumatic Growth 148
Power Posing 169

Prison 111
Problems sleeping 128
Psychotherapeutic Approaches 155
PTSD Treatments 155
Reliving the past 133
Resilience 152
Re-Traumatization 121
Revenge 133
Roger Callahan 35
Ronald A Ruden 156
School 111
Self-Medication 133
Self Tapping 46
Sexual Abuse 134
Shaking 61
Shame 128
Single Event Trauma 121
Skype 74
Sleepiness 61
Snowball of Stress 122
Somatic Poem 97
Song and Dance 99
Stress 119
Stress Symptoms 132
SUD 54
Suicide 133
Summary Trauma 121
Sweating 61
Sympathetic nervous system 119
Sympathizing 149
Tapping Somebody 66
Tension in muscles 133
Thoughts 127
Tired 133
Transferability 110
Trauma 119
Trauma Tapping Centers 183
Trauma Tapping Technique 45
TRE 156
Triggered Symptoms 132
TTT on the Fly 77
TTT with Hypnotherapy 82

Tunnel vision 120
Ulf Sandström 11
9 gamut 165

Books for references and inspiration

A long way gone, Ishmael Beah, Harper Perennial, 2008

A Time for New Dreams, Ben Okri, Rider, 2011

Awareness, The Perils and Opportunities of Reality, Anthony de Mello, Image Books, Doubleday, 1992

Black Swan: The Impact of the Highly Improbable, Nassim Nicholas Taleb, Random House Trade, 2010

Clean Laguage, Judy Rees, Wendy Sullivan, Crown House Publishing, 2008

Dancing in the Glory of Monsters, Jason Stearns, PublicAffairs, 2012

David vs Goliath: Underdogs, Misfits, and the Art of Battling Giants, Malcolm Gladwell, Little, Brown & Company Hachette Book Group, 2013

Energy Medicine: How to use Your Body Energies for Optimum Health and Vitality, Donna Eden and David Feinstein, Piatkus Books, 2008

Energy Tapping for Trauma, Fred Gallo, New Harbinger Publications, 2007

Everything you need to know to feel Go(o)d, Candace Pert, Hay House Inc, 2007

Four Hour Work Week, Timothy Ferris, Vermilion, 2011

Getting Past Your Past – Take Control of Your Life With Self-Help Techniques from EMDR, Francine Shapiro, Rodale Incorporated, 2013

Healing Trauma, Peter Levine, Sounds True, 2008

Indian Handbook of Hypnotherapy, Drs Bhaskar and Rajni Vyas, Concept Publishing, 2009

King Leopold's Ghost, Adam Hochschild, Mariner Books, 1998

Managing Groups – The Inside Track from Good to Great, Michael Grinder, Michael Grinder & Associates, 2008

Mapping The Mind, Rita Carter, Phoenix, 2010

Mindfulness Meditation for Everyday Life, Jon Kabat Zinn, Piatkus, Judy Publishers, 1994

Molecules of Emotion – Why you feel the Way you feel, Candace Pert, Scribner Book Company, 1999

Peace is Every Step, Thich Nhat Hanh, Bantam Books, 1992

Stop The Nightmares of Trauma: Thought Field Therapy, the Power Therapy for the 21st Century, Roger Callahan, 2000

Sway: The Irresistible Pull of Irrational Behaviour, Ori & Brom Brafman, Broadway Business, 2009

Tao Teh King, Lao zi, translation by Aleister Crowley, Askin Publishers, 1976

Tapping the Healer Within, Roger Callahan, McGraw-Hill Contemporary, 2002

The Antelope's Strategy: Living in Rwanda After the Genocide, Jean Hatzfeld, Picador, 2010

The Big Book of NLP Techniques, Shlomo Vaknin, 2008

The Biology of Belief – Unleashing the Power of Counsciousness, Matter & Miracles, Bruce Lipton, Hay House Inc, 2011

Heart of Darkness, Joseph Conrad, 1899

The Healing Wisdom of Africa, Malidoma Patrice Somé, Tarcher, 1999

The Logic of Life, Tim Harford, Abacus, 2009

The Long Road Turns to Joy, Thich Nhat Hanh, Full Circle, 1996

The Origins of Neurolinguistic Programming, edited by John Grinder, Frank Pucelik, Crown House Publishing Ltd, 2013

The Power of Now, Eckhart Tolle, Hodder Paperback, 2005

The Promise of Energy Psychology, David Feinstein, Donna Eden, Gary Craig, Tarcher/Penguin, 2005

The Rainbow Machine, Andrew Austin, Real People Press, 2007

The Survivors Club, Ben Sherwood, Hachette UK, 2009

The Way to Happiness, Dalai Lama and Howard C. Cutler, 1998

The Wisdom of no Escape and the Path of Loving Kindness, Pema Chödrön, Shambala Classics, 1992

Waking the Tiger, Healing Trauma, Dr. Peter Levine, North Atlantic Books, 1997

We wish to inform you that tomorrow we will be killed with our families, Philip Gourevitch, Picador, 2000

What is the What, Dave Eggers, McSweeney's, 2007

When the Past is Always Present – Emotional Traumatization, Causes and Cures, Dr. Ronald A. Ruden, Taylor & Francis, 2010

Where There is No Doctor – A Village Care Handbook, David Werner, Carol Thuman, Jane Maxwell, Macmillan Education Ltd, Edition of 1993

"Thank You"

With love
Gunilla Hamne and Ulf Sandström

For more information see
www.peacefulheart.se